~~~

I JUST WANT MY DAUGHTER BACK

A heartfelt story of a mother's struggle to overcome fear, confusion, anger, guilt and frustration in the midst of her daughter's battle with a devastating mental illness. How we came to terms through love, courage, perseverance and hope as we struggled to learn how to live with Bipolar-1 Disorder.

B.C. Levinson

This is a work of non-fiction. Character's names outside of immediate family have been modified to protect their anonymity. All other names are accurate and events are written to the best of my knowledge and memory.

Library of Congress Cataloging-in-Publication

ISBN : 144213979X

EAN-13 : 9781442139794

Printed and Published in the United States of America

Additional information, please contact
MAMA_BEAR_CLUB@yahoo.com

For my grandson, who has brought such immense joy to my life and brought us through a time when joy was something needed so greatly.   Thank you for being a constant precious miracle. I cherish you most of all.

For my daughter, who continually inspires and motivates me in my own struggle with the insignificant burdens of my world. Thank you for understanding my many failures and appreciating my heartfelt efforts. You make me so proud.

TABLE OF CONTENTS

CHAPTER 1   August 1999

Saturdays are my oasis, a reprieve from the incessant heat of another week at work. Sleeping later than usual, sitting on my back porch and slowly sipping coffee is my way of finding balance. Days where there's no problems to solve, no crisis that can't wait. Saturdays I'm usually just like a kite, floating in the breeze but this morning nothing seems to be going right, somehow things feel tense and scattered, all at the same time.

As I climb the stairs to check in on Steph, the quietness in her room makes me uneasy. As I reach the top of the stairs, I notice the usually sparse living area is cluttered with what appears to be, most of her belongings. I'm bewildered by the lack of neatness that has always been her trademark. Stepping over piles of crumpled clothes and a homecoming corsage that has held a prominent place on her bulletin board for almost a year; I approach the darkened corner room. Having two teenagers, the lack of commotion only magnifies the quiet stillness- moms just know silence can be deafening.

"Steph honey, are you up yet?" Peering inside, I scan the walls and shelves. For a moment, I assume she must be reorganizing her room again. Gradually, I become aware of the emptiness of what was once a perfectionist dream. It feels odd to me that her favorite comforter is bunched up in the far corner, but a closer look reveals messy strands of chestnut hair and one white knuckled hand.

Standing there in her doorway, I almost miss her clutching the comforter like her life depends on it. Staring off into space, she is mumbling, her eyes as vacant as her room, saying nothing and everything. For a moment, it feels like I have walked into someone else's room, that I am looking at a stranger. I stand there blinking, looking around to find something that reveals some sense of normalcy. Nothing about this picture seems right in my mind, only the corsage and the familiar comforter pull me back to certainty. In this moment, on this Saturday, I know Steph has slipped away, to where, I don't know—but I would do anything to get her back. Seeing her so out of her element, trembling uncontrollably, I realize I don't know who is frightened more, me or my little girl.

This particular Saturday will always make me think of a fierce storm. Warnings are always given but like many who get caught off guard, I've ignored them. I didn't understand the magnitude of the danger it could bring, I'm still not sure what is happening. Now as I'm staring in the face of this storm, I can feel its power tearing and twisting at my papier-mâché fortress. Our lives are crumbling before my eyes and I don't know where to turn.

Despite all the warnings, I find myself totally unprepared for the devastation this storm is bringing to my home. Being an accountant and office manager, analyzing and solving problems come easy for me so this shouldn't have caught me by surprise, but it did. Even the phrase there's a method to my madness annoys me. I'd rather just eliminate the madness. Of course when it comes to my daughter, to do away with the madness I must first acknowledge the chaos. Denial can be such a potent word.

All my life I have been told that there are solutions to all problems. Yet, I have somehow failed to see that there is a problem even as it unfolds before my eyes. Well, that's not entirely true, strange occurrences have become commonplace for quite a while. It's just that my inability to accept Steph's uncharacteristic behaviors lately has steadily paralyzed me into uncertainty, something I don't readily like to admit.

2

The world is crashing down around me; I can't breathe or even think straight. Every parent goes through periods of denial when their mind tells them something is going wrong but their heart says "no- not my child, it will pass." The saying "Love is Blind" often applies to not only those of us who are love sick in a rocky relationship, but also to mothers and fathers of children with problems you as a parent can't see objectively. Often times you will be the last one to accept the reality of coming truths.

Recently, I have struggled with the thought that maybe I'm just a panic-stricken mom, clinging to control as my daughter reaches for independence, that I'm making a mountain out of a mole hill. I have convinced myself it's just a strange phase she is going through; still I should have taken a closer look. I've had to fend off hundreds of pressing questions and comments lately. Now, I suspect those warning signs should have been much more obvious than I've wanted to admit. Stubbornly, I've held on to the belief that nothing was really wrong, not with Steph, it will pass.

And now that my world is in chaos, the sheer gravity of it has slapped me in the face; my mind is forced to see things as they are. It has only become more confusing, desperation is setting in. Then, just as my mind begins to inch ahead of my heart, seeing things with a bit more clarity, I find I no longer trust my own instincts as a parent. When you know something is going horribly wrong with a loved ones mind, how do our instincts react?

Instinct has played an enormous role in all humanity since the beginning of time. We are all born with these impulses that are designed to help us survive as a species. Behavior patterns that do not appear to have been learned kick in magically, by some unknown trigger. But are they really magical or is it through trial and error that we learn to act subconsciously, only repeating what works?

These types of instincts can easily be observed in a variety of examples. The fight or flight response is a result of

3

an adrenaline surge our body instinctively sends to help us combat threats. The craving of high calorie foods has been instinctively developed over millions of years simply to insure the survival of our most fit species. Babies use the simple instinctive tactic of crying to get parents to jump to the rescue, insuring their needs are met. Our overwhelming desires to procreate, nurture, protect and safeguard our children have all developed as instinctive behaviors in order to secure future human existence.

But do we have the instincts we need to respond to situations so completely out of our realm, such as mental illness. I know some of the instilled responses can be an enormous help to me as I grope for direction. However, I have also been designed with instinctive emotions which govern my heart, sometimes getting in the way of my logic thought. These feelings and impulses are colliding in a frantic jumble, making it difficult for me to sort through this crisis in a logical manner. In the midst of this nightmare, can I know how to hold on to my own sense of reality?

This has come out of nowhere—Crazy, Looney, Nuts, Twisted, Psycho—you name it, I'm thinking it. I know someone is not of sound mind, but which one of us is it? I don't think I have the instincts needed to deal with an issue so completely out of my realm; I'm not at all sure what the issue even is. What I do know now, in this moment, something is horribly wrong with my daughters mind. This thought is so foreign to me, so unknown to me, my emotions are suffocating me.

All these emotions cloud my mind, then like a life raft, somewhere in the midst this turbulent nightmare my mind drifts to phrases from my past. They're just words, but I want to cling to them the same way Steph is clinging to her comforter. The same way my family has always clung to these phrases to survive life's storms. Phrases my parents have taught us that have become such a mainstay in our lives for years. So I tell myself that is what I must continue to do, to cling to those precious words.

4

Like most mothers, after a little practice I quickly began to look at myself as the fix-it Mom, the go to gal. My baby gets hurt, and I'm there with a kiss, bottle of peroxide and a band-aid to make it all better. Just tell me someone hurt my child and I become the Mama Bear no one would ever want to encounter. You've got a question, I've got answers. I'm the twentieth century heroine of the world, and the conquering leader of troubling times. I'm the epitome of the super-mom. That is, until I stepped out of the fog and see how utterly lost I am, see how totally helpless and clueless I am, as I did today.

What would have prepared me for the greatest challenge of my life? Oh I've had my share of trails and troubles, suffered loss in one form or another as much as anyone I guess. And like most people, I found ways to deal with them. Although I must admit sometimes it seems more in spite of me as much as through my own efforts. But this is not a topic that was covered in those baby classes I took. In the entire library, amongst all those books about baby names, how to raise an obedient child, what to feed them, how not to spank them, toilet training and breast feeding, where does it explain how I as a parent, can cope with my child's mental illness?

I don't know where to turn. Who can understand what's happening? I certainly don't. I'm not sure I can even remotely describe what's happening. Is there anyone out there that can tell me what's going on? And if you're out there, how will I find you? If I find you, how will I be confident of anything you say? I need someone to tell me what to do.

Anger, fear, confusion, frustration, panic, resentment, disappointment, hopelessness, these and many other varieties of emotions are flying through me all at once. I must look like a chicken with its head cut off, running around the farm yard, or one of the salmon of the northwest trying to swim upstream in an attempt to reach an unfathomable goal.

5

Nevertheless, I instinctively know in my heart, I must remain the rock, the safety net and protector, because someone more important to me than all the gold in Fort Knox will need me to stand with her. I must never tire, never stop seeking answers, never leave her unsupported, always be conscientious of my reactions and most of all never ever turn my back. I will do all these things gladly with my whole heart and soul.

What I didn't expect was that the path on which I was about to embark would be the emotional equivalent of climbing Mount Everest. I only wish there was a manuscript to follow, an instruction book to use as a guide, even a small check list that will give me the direction I am so apparently lacking.

We parents all have trials and heartaches in the course of raising our children. With the rise in mental health issues in our country, you may have found yourself in my shoes. My heart goes out to you with a sense of camaraderie for the continual anguish we share. My purpose in telling this story is not to advise or suggest in any way that I know the answers to your questions relating to these illnesses. I only want to communicate that you are not alone in your suffering and uncertainty. I want to share with you a sense of hope and inspiration that is so desperately needed to survive this type of crisis.

I am not a doctor or psychiatrist nor do I have any medical training. I'm just a Mom, a mom with a child in a crisis. I have thought a lot in the past few years about the importance of telling Stephanie's story. Knowing what I know now, seeing what I've seen, understanding things a little better now, I have decided it is just the right time.

Selfishly, I believe this adventure may be therapeutic for me. As if putting it all down in print will wash away some of the frustration I have set aside this past decade. I'm not at all confident I can put my thoughts to paper, in a manner that will have any clarity for you, as a reader. This story makes little sense to me some days, with confusion and self-doubt reining over my world so much in these past years. But I will endeavor to pour from my heart the account of this challenge as best I can. Maybe it will give us both a better perspective if, I start from the beginning.

CHAPTER 2   March 1981

Nothing beats hearing the pediatrician say, "You have a healthy seven-and-a-half pound girl, all fingers and toes present and accounted for." After a long nine months of pregnancy and eighteen hours of labor, I can finally put those stressful months of uncertainty and worry aside and just enjoy motherhood for the first time. All mothers go through an assortment of self-doubts, endure weird nightmares, and spend countless hours watching everything we eat, drink, breath and smell in order to do our part in the miracle of creation. Now that day is here and I can sit back and take pleasure in the blissful joy of my new arrival. I've done a good job, mission accomplished. How very proud I am, right?

I discover that feeling only lasts until about the time they wheel me out to the car, where I am supposed to place my bundle of joy in her new car seat. Hum…. standing there, looking at that contraption, confusion comes over me as reality sets in. I look over to my husband, Mike, for reassurance only to see a mirror image of my own apprehension. His dark hair and beard covering most of the paleness that shadows over his round dimpled face, only deep worry lines betray his inner thoughts. Though married just three years, I have already learned that he will keep those thoughts to himself. Always ready to listen and analyze other's problems, he rarely opens up, exposing his own inner fears or frustration.

As my mind wanders, I find myself thinking of those sweet nurses back upstairs. After two days of watching them, handling a dozen babies at a time in the nursery, I wish one of

9

them was coming home with me. I can't help thinking that I'm really not equipped for this. Will I know how to handle any of the numerous situations that are now flooding my mind?

I've read every book I could get my hands on, asked 15 million questions, watched tapes for hours, took all the appropriate baby classes and purchased enough supplies for a small daycare. Yet somehow, now I can't seem to figure out how to even strap my little one in her car seat. She obviously picks up on my uncertainty, my lack of expertise and begins to express herself in the only way a two day old baby knows. Now I want my mommy. What was I thinking? At twenty-three, I'm barely out of childhood myself. Gratefully, I allow the nurse to assist me and crisis number one is averted, the first of which I am now suspecting will be in the neighborhood of around one hundred million by her high school graduation.

Days and weeks pass and I find myself discovering that I apparently do have enough competency to feed, bathe, diapers, and put my daughter down to sleep. It also helps that Stephanie seems to enjoy sleeping like Rip Van Winkle and nursing like Porky the Pig (of course in the most delicate way). The diaper thing is not nearly as pleasant as it was in baby class or as simple (they really should let you practice with spastic robotic dolls). Giving her a bath, with her slippery body sliding around in her new baby tub, I quickly conclude there is good reason to always buy the "no more tears" shampoo.

In spite of my feelings of inadequacy, with practice, perseverance and some wise counsel from my own Mama we muddle through, settling into a routine that becomes somewhat like second nature. What I see as my accomplishments each day is giving me a newly found confidence. Hey, this isn't so difficult; maybe Mama is right after all in telling me, "just stay calm, take one step at a time, don't be so independent you refuse to ask for guidance and for God's sake, use some common sense"

Now that I have a child, I am just beginning to appreciate my mother, Katherine, just beginning to reflect on, who she really is. I have a black and white studio headshot taken back in the late forties of her when she was just becoming an adult. Her short dark hair is done in the wavy style of the times, combed back off her small oval face. With not even a hint of a smile, she is looking off to her left; her large eyes have a sad yet serene, accepting look about them. It somehow gives the impression of an apprehensive deer, tells me that she is not quite sure of herself, of who she is just yet. This photo makes me wonder how she grew from that timid young lady into the self confident woman I now look to for advice.

All my life I've witnessed this woman doing things others would shy away from with uncanny confidence and a positive attitude. I grew up watching her approach every problem, task, chore, or project that arose with one of her favorite sentences; "come on, let's try, it can't be that hard." I can remember how fearless Mama was when it came to tackling wallpapering, painting, recovering sofas, and all sorts of projects that came up around the house. Nothing ever seems to overwhelm her, "just take one step at a time".

Why have I not really noticed these things or even considered what makes her that way? Looking at that picture, I get the impression she didn't start out that way. Having a child myself now, being unsure of myself, feeling a little lost, I realize I want to understand her secrets and apply them in the hope that I too can grow, can become more than I am. Do all young mothers suddenly have this epiphany or have I just become aware that I was not paying attention to lessons taught as I was growing up?

I think a lot about my daughter and the role I must play. I don't want her to feel lost as she enters adulthood and so, I commit myself to discovering those secrets from Mama. Then, hopefully I can pass that knowledge on to my own daughter, who daily seems to be eagerly soaking up everything like a sponge. Maybe that will make the difference; even as a baby she just seems so eager to discover the mysteries of the world.

Steph enjoys spending time just contently lying there in her crib, eyes absorbed in the colors and patterns of her curtains. After careful study of each detail she moves her attention to the wallpaper then to her mobile of animals hanging over her crib. As I watch her intently examine each item, I almost feel left out, like I'm not really needed. Oh, I know she does, for things she obviously can't do for herself like a diaper change or a feeding, but the feeling is still there just under the surface. We can go on for hours this way, her examining and I, just watching in amazement at her scrutiny. Then as she gets hungry, she begins to fuss, not cry, only soft whimpers, like she just knows I'll be there waiting to nurse her.

It's only been a few weeks since bringing her home, yet Mike and I several times a night slip through the dark apartment into her room just to make sure she is okay. Sometimes if we can't tell if she is breathing, we nudge her ever so slightly so she moves on her own. I know it sounds silly, but we can't believe our daughter is sleeping such long stretches when everyone we know has remarked on how often they had to get up at night.

Most people say you can't tell which parent a baby favors until they are much older, but we don't want to buy in to this notion. Mike proudly declares "she obviously gets the round face, dimples and dark hair from me" and I lay claim to her large long lashed hazel eyes. When she smiles the whole room seems to light up just with her presence. As she learns to giggle, I can't help but think of the Pillsbury Dough Boy from the TV commercials as I squeeze her chubby little arms and legs. Mike claims instead "no it's the Michelin Girl, just look at her tire rolls stacked on her arms and legs". It figures, only a guy would think of that. I just don't see how she can be so delicately dainty and plump at the same time. It's beyond me.

12

Mike and I jealously bicker from time to time over who gets to take her to the store. Each of us will firmly stand our ground in the living room of our small apartment stubbornly laying claim to the prize. All smiles and giggles, we both delight in the outings as she often holds up the trips attracting and amusing fellow shoppers. Over and over, she sits in the seat of the grocery cart searching for someone to make contact with. She stares them down until they notice her, and then burst into giggles, kicking her tiny pink painted toes, waving her chubby little hands at them.

As she gets older, I love watching her and her father go off together. Mike, so proud of the little girl who in many ways does look so much like him, boldly takes her everywhere with him and Steph gladly goes along. Relishing her independence from me now that I have weaned her, all I get is a giggle and a wave goodbye. After almost a year of breastfeeding her, feeling so connected to her, I get the impression that this is my first glimpse of what it feels like, letting go, letting her soar on her own. I'm not so sure I like this feeling. I get the sense that I will struggle with this feeling always, even though I know in my heart, raising a child is surrounded by this very process.

As Mike and Steph are leaving together, I have a flashback to my own childhood. Only eight or nine years old, I'm up in my usual perch, high in the mimosa tree in our front yard waiting for my Daddy, Olen, to arrive home from his job at a manufacturing plant. Mama told me almost an hour ago "Your Daddy won't be working late tonight; He's on his way home". Excitement fills the air the moment he comes around the corner and pulls into the drive. His blonde crew cut is glistening with sweat in the late afternoon sun, grey eyes shaded by his big brown sunglasses. He slowly rolls the window up, grabs the work he has brought home and gets out of his old blue Pontiac. Just as he passes around the front of the car, I dangle down before him; he jumps back in mock surprise, as I giggle with glee. "You got me again" he says as he reaches into his pocket for a stick of Big Red that he keeps just for this occasion.

13

It's a game we play; only I am still too young to realize it. Still too young to realize that he has a special unique way to make all four of his children feel like they are each his favorite. It will be many years before I catch on to the notion that Daddy has the ability to make everyone he comes in contact with, feel special. Years before I mature enough to grasp his own special uniqueness. Now, I'm just a little girl filled with joy, just sharing this moment with the one man I love. As I remember those moments, I smile, believing Steph will grow up feeling that same joy.

As Steph grows, I gain an overwhelming sense of pride as she soars above all the latest childhood development charts. Conquering each milestone with blazing speed and agility, I am amazed by her resourcefulness and determination. There she will sit, at her little table for hours; patiently putting puzzles together, never frustrated, just busy analyzing each piece before finding the proper placement. She smiles with satisfaction, then dumps the puzzle out and only to begin again.

I am aware that I'm not the first mother who thinks her child must be advanced for her age and possibly the potential yet-to-be- discovered prodigy. I don't think all this boasting is such a bad thing, considering my little one is more than likely to overhear the discussions. I believe I am actually helping her to develop a positive sense of self esteem and self worth. I believe it's our duty as parents to shout from the mountaintop that our pride and joy is the dearest thing to our hearts. I seem to be more than happy to fulfill the role.

Very late one night we get a phone call, Daddy has been rushed to the hospital. After a relaxing vacation, he was to return to his stressful new management position at the plant in the morning. Mike and I scoop Steph up from her bed and hurry to the emergency room. We find Mama in the corridor stoically waiting for the doctor. "A massive myocardial infarction" he tells us "but we haven't discovered the cause yet. His heart is enlarged with a large amount of fluid in the sack surrounding it."

14

It takes me a minute to realize the doctor is taking about a major heart attack. This does not seem possible; Daddy has the heart of a lion. Always exhibiting a quiet strength, he has always been a constant force in all our lives. How can this happen to someone so invincible?

Weeks pass as he remains in intensive care, his heart palpitating rapidly every time Mama leaves the room. I never thought much until now about the strong connection they shared, how dependent they were on each other, relying on each other's strengths to get them through the tough times. They just always seem to me to be as one, a solid wall standing together in all things.

One day Mama needs to run home for a few minutes so, I stay in the room with him while he sleeps. Not long after she leaves, he wakes up and weakly calls, "Is that you?" I lean over him and quietly say, "It's me, I thought you were sleeping." At the sound of my voice, looking over at me, he relaxes back on his pillow and says, "Forgot where I was Kat, can't believe I'm still so weak."

As I just stood there for a moment, stunned, I think to myself, "He thinks I'm Mama". He's always told me, I was the spitting image of Mama. I find myself proud of the fact that he has mistaken me for her. Patting his arm and I tell him "just try to rest, it will get better." Not long after, Mama returns almost in a panic until she sees that he's fine. The relief on her face tells all.

Daddy remains in the hospital for six weeks, by time he returns to work more than three months has passed. Since he hasn't missed more than one day of work in more than 20 years, his accumulated sick time more than covers his salary, reaffirming his belief that determination and dedication pay's off.

Once back at work, more than ever, Mama watches him like a hawk. I simply find myself smiling at the role models I have been blessed with, smile at the thought that

15

Steph will grow up surrounded by such well grounded loved ones. I make a mental note to point out to her as she grows up, all of the wonderful things that make them who they are.

Steph's first birthday arrives and so do her words. Talking, talking, and talking. Now I know my sweet little girl is saying the usual first words of all children, probably right on schedule. Nothing is unusually gifted in her early vocabulary. It's just Steph seems to really enjoy talking; she seems to have an overwhelming desire to communicate to everyone about everything, all day long. Whether we are at home or in the car, it is always the same. "Mom" she says "those birds are pretty." "Where are they going?" "Maybe they're hungry." "I'm hungry too." "I want to eat." "Where's Dad?" "Can we have Mac-n-cheese?" "Birds are funny." It never stops.

Though I am amazed at how quickly she moved to full sentences, I think it is her clarity of speech that surprises me most. I have always had such trouble deciphering other children's babble; with Steph it's so simple. At first I think it is just a mother's instinct to understand their own child's communications but others continually comment on her proficiency. Each word is pronounced properly and most often in the correct context. Steph is quickly becoming the twin to the Chatty Kathy Doll—minus the pull string. Sometimes, I have to admit, I wish for the pull string.

No longer do I believe the success I feel, is in any way due to my accomplishments as such a great mother. I know it's primarily due to Stephanie being an extremely easy baby and I am simply here to just stick to her self-imposed schedule and enjoy the ride.

And enjoy the ride I have, so much so, I must have unconsciously decided to have another child. Now I must be off my rocker! Why mess with perfection? It's not like I don't already have enough to worry about? My little dream child is only thirteen months old and I'm pregnant with what I am now desperately hoping is another easy baby.

Though I feel a little panicked, Mama simply reminds me "you're not the first one to have two small children in diapers, just take a deep breath and take one step at a time. When you're feeling overwhelmed, just remember, this too shall pass."

As I take to heart these words, I find they have a calming effect. I've heard this advice throughout my life but now I'm really listening to the truth of these words. I'm beginning to realize, this just might be how Mama made the great transformation.

The next nine months seem to fly by with lightning speed. As I prepare for the next arrival, my no-longer-little bundle of joy is mastering countless skills, moving from crawling to walking to grabbing everything in sight for a thorough hand to mouth inspection. Her ability to find the most miniscule items is almost as surprising as her fascination with them.

Who are these people who think small children can't distinguish right from wrong. They obviously have not had to run from the other side of the room in attempt to stop their child from putting who knows what in their mouths. It's only when the child realizes their mommy sees them that the race is on.

As most mothers expecting their second child would do, I am trying to prepare my daughter for the arrival of what I already know (thanks to the frequent use of the sonogram) to be her little brother. Several times a day I tell her "what a big girl you are now, Mom will need your help with baby brother". She is catching on to the idea like a miniature Einstein, inspired by the prospect that she will be the backup mommy. To me she seems to be transforming from a baby to a little girl almost overnight.

I imagine Steph growing up; worries escalate with the self-realization that I am not at all prepared for the task at hand. My heart aches with mixed emotions; one part of me

17

wants her to always be my little baby girl, while the other part recognizes my duty in this venture is to help her one day become a strong independent young woman.

Parenthood is such an exciting time for me; just seeing all these transformations is the most captivating experience of my life, full of amazing adventures. It seems every few months as I think to myself that this is my favorite age, only a few months go by and I must rethink that mindset, as she grows and becomes more fascinating.

Though I am trying to be the most careful parent, sometimes the most terrifying things can still happen. It's a typical hot august day in Texas, only 102 degrees and being almost five months pregnant, I'm sure feeling the heat. I need to stop and get gas, a visit to the bathroom would be nice, but with Steph asleep in the back seat, that will have to wait. I wish I didn't have to shut the car and consequently the a/c, off; instead I think, "I'll just have to be quick about it."

As I fill the car the up, my little stinker wakes up, unbuckles her own seat and climbs out. "I'm going to have to find a way to curb this clever trait", I think to myself. I tap on the back window and tell her, "Steph, honey, get back in your seat" but no, instead she reaches over to play with the door lock. The thump of the lock seems so loud it drowns out all traffic noise.

Now I'm panicked, running around to each of the windows on the car trying to convince Steph to pull up on the door lock. She finds the chocolate candy I have left in the front console much more fascinating. As she settles into to the front passenger seat to enjoy her new found treat, I find myself just standing there in disbelief as I watch beads of sweet slowly trickle down her face.

The station attendant calls to me, "Hey lady, I just called the fire department. They'll have that open in no time." That's Texas for you; people are always looking out for each other. "It's the pregnancy, my daughter did that very same

18

thing when she was carrying her second child" says a small framed lady about my own mother's age. As she pats me on the shoulder, she continues, "The trick is to always keep your keys in your hand". I try to smile as the tears and sweat mingle together on their trek down my cheek.

In moments, the sound of those sirens blaring as they raced towards us became the most beautiful sound imaginable. Two firemen come over to my car and quickly assess the situation, as predicted in no time they have the door open. Steph, covered in sweat and chocolate, giggles as she is passed from one of the firemen to me. As relief floods over me, I'm left wondering if I will always be such a scatter brain and how well am I going to be able manage two of these little stinker's.

For the rest of my days I promise myself I will always pump my gas with my keys in my hand. As for the too easy to work car seat; thankfully only a few year's will pass before car seat manufacturers begin to make the contraptions so difficult to operate, grandmother's all across America will need countless sessions of instruction on how to operate the blasted things!

The exact day my daughter becomes 21 months of age we welcome our eight-and-a-half pound little boy, Phillip, into our world. When we bring "Brother" (the only name she will call him for years) home from the hospital, Steph is so excited to get started doing her part.

I am so relieved in those first weeks to see her blossom into the perfect little assistant to mommy as anyone with more than one small child at home would be. Oh, the doubts, anxiety and fears still pop up here and there but I've done this once already, it can't be that hard. Or so I remind myself as I remember Mama's words as I struggle with two children under the age of two.

After several weeks of sending sister for Brother's baby diapers my big girl decides she's too grown up for those things now. "I want to use Mommy's potty, I'm a big girl" Steph says as she declines to use the typical toddler potty we had purchased. Instead she pushes her stool over to climb up onto the big toilet just like me. Hmmm…, that was much easier than I thought it would be but, then again everything else with her has been pretty much a walk in the park, why not toilet training? So I get her big girl panties and we're off to the races! And yes, surprisingly even through the night.

She is determined to grow up fast, easily tackling everything from vocabulary to doing everything for herself. I am amazed at her resolute mindset and good natured attitude about all she confronts. Always analytical and decisive, Steph patiently dissects every task at hand and finds the most efficient and practical solution to each problem.

Nothing seems to frustrate her or be to complicated for her, whether it be attempting to memorize small verses, spelling small words with blocks, or adding the number of toys laid out for her to count. As I look into their bedroom, I am not surprised to find her once again patiently holding a mock school class. It is so cute watching her play with Brother and the four other children that I now baby sit to make extra money, as she attempts to teach them everything within her knowledge.

I'm beginning to understand how important these early years of child development really are. I've heard over and over that this is when their character and values are instilled in them. Teaching them patience, self control and perseverance are some of the most valuable lessons parents can teach our future adults.

Mama is very wise to constantly advise her children that "most things are not as hard as we think, take one step at a time, keep moving one foot in front of the other and always remember….. this too shall pass." I am beginning to understand the importance of these sentiments, the value they can bring to our lives and want to share them with my own children. Isn't it peculiar that as we become parents we suddenly recognize that our own mothers and fathers are much more intelligent than we had previously thought?

Being big sister is the central focus of Stephanie's life. Mike and I love watching her keeping an eye out for Brother, helping him with everything from putting on his shoes to coloring. Steph seems to be evolving into a miniature mommy, always patient, thoughtful and kind; she worries and fusses over him like a mother hen. I wonder is my own worry wart behavior something I'm subconsciously teaching her as she tries to imitate me.

As a parent, I recognize I'm a bit of a worrier and even stress needlessly over pretty inconsequential things sometimes. But isn't that what we are supposed to do as parents? From the moment that new life is created, we feel an enormous responsibility for and take to heart our duty to care for, nourish, and protect what has been placed in our charge?

It is built into us genetically, passed on by millions of years of refining and sustaining our species. Judging from my worrisome personality, my genes must be substantially fine tuned, probably even excessively so. How is it I can have the tendency to take small things and blow them completely out of proportion such as turning a simple thing like a trip to the mall into a national security crisis?

We have all experienced it; the panic felt when you discover as you are tending to the one child in the stroller the other one hides behind the clothes rack for a minute. You just know they have been abducted! Or the fear that creeps into your heart as your child is playing happily at the park and you see them dangling high on the Jungle Gym looking like they are about to fall.

Then there's the uncertainty and self doubt you have over the numerous decisions you are now required to make regarding their wellbeing. These mixed feelings all seem never ending and countless to me yet by no means interfere with the joy, tenderness and pride I experience day by day.

21

During Steph's early years I learn to weigh my emotions against logic. I'm doing the best I can, to keep my apprehension in check. I want to just take pleasure in watching her thriving personality form into a charming, helpful, compassionate, determined and intelligent little girl.

I become accustom to her always flourishing in school and being blessed with perpetual good health, rarely suffering from so much as a cold. My focus and worries are now diverted to Phillip. He is continually afflicted with a variety of illnesses ranging from earaches and colds which, more often than not develop, into bronchitis. It is as if the timeless adage "the squeaky wheel always gets the oil" attempting to prove a point through my son.

After years of disconnect, Mike and I divorce just as Steph enters the second grade. She appears to take it all in stride as if in an unconscious attempt to put my guilt and shame at ease for disrupting our family. Her ability to adjust to whatever circumstance arises is comforting, and also alleviates much of my own anxiety. It is as though she perceives my own need for reassurance that I am not damaging her sense of wellbeing. Then again, sometimes I have the feeling that I'm turning a blind eye in an attempt to diminish the anguish I feel over my contribution to the turmoil in our lives.

Mike and I both focus on rebuilding our lives, each separately making our way in the world, trying to find a new sense of normalcy. I find myself returning to the work force for the first time in years. I struggle with separation trauma as I find myself having so little time with my children. They have been my whole life and the new added requirement of having my own apartment, paying my own bills sometimes takes its toll on my emotions.

As the years pass Steph seems to be soaring through time scarcely taking a moment to just be a little girl. Always the miniature grown up she rarely causes a moment's concern, content to look after Brother no matter if it's at

Moms or Dads. She eagerly takes over doing her own laundry as well as Brother's and quickly learns how to prepare simple meals.

Most of the time it is Steph who gives assistance to Phillip in completing and checking his homework as well as in helping him clean his room. When he is upset about something he typically goes to her for comforting as well as any guidance he feels he needs. I often feel out of the loop by their little twosome but am comforted that they are so close and only hoping that it would continue throughout their lives.

Dealing with most situations with a maturity well beyond her years, Steph's mindset and attitudes about life's obstacle course of circumstances give me an assurance that she is growing into a well adjusted, strong and resilient young lady developing the abilities to triumph over any challenges of her world.

CHAPTER 3   Spring 1995

While sitting at my desk at work I listen to coworkers complain about their teenage daughters developing sassy mouths, laziness with chores, fondness for inappropriate clothing and rebellious attitudes and wonder how I am so fortunate as to be missing out on these frustrating encounters.

Part of me smugly wants to take recognition for Steph's smooth transition into adolescence, while parental pride compels me to give credit where credit's due; after all, it's her behavior showing such exemplary perfection. I smile as I realize my memories of these years will include pleasant things such as cooking dinner together, easy talks as we do various chores together, long quarrel-free shopping trips and cheerful hugs as Steph heads off for school. Her sense of responsibility is demonstrated daily as she uses her own alarm clock to get up for school, completes many chores around the house without prompting and self manages all her school assignments.

As I drive home from my new accounting job at the Surveying and Engineering Firm where I now work, traffic is heavy; people can be so impatient. The a/c in my car aggravates me even more, as I realize I will need to have that checked before summer fully arrives. Pulling into the drive I take a deep breath, preparing myself for an evening of chores that I know need to be dealt with.

As I enter through the laundry room, I find several loads of clothes separated by colors on the floor waiting their turn. The clinking of pans explains the delicious aroma that is floating to me from the kitchen.

Rounding the corner I find Steph, holding a steaming pan she just removed from the oven. "Hi Mom," she chirps, smiling radiantly, "thought I'd try a new meatloaf recipe." "Did you have another crazy day?" Just seeing her standing there, takes the hours of frustration off my shoulders. "Yea, well nothing too tragic. That smells good" I reply. As she sets the pan on the counter she waves me on my way saying, "It'll be ready in a bit, go change."

As I head for my bedroom to change from my work clothes, I notice once again she has vacuumed and straightened up the living room. What is it that makes her seem to enjoy being so grown up? Possibly the years of being left in charge have ingrained in her a sense of duty to keep the fire going at home while her parents are at work.

It's easy to see why I am so accustom to never worrying about her, Steph always seems so in control of her world as well as the universe around her. And there is always her brother who needs my attention so much more. True, Phillip is not sick very often anymore, but his attention to schoolwork is always lacking and let's just says he doesn't seem to be as eager to grow up as his sister.

It takes a conscious effort for me not to always compare him in my mind to her. I remind myself that they are unique people with different strengths, weaknesses, and maturity levels. I just need to be patient and understanding, letting him come into his own at his own pace. I admit it, I am spoiled.

A friend of mine is always reminding me, "Steph is not the typical girl and Phillip definitely is behaving as all little boys normally do". She tries to keep me grounded in the thought of not putting too much pressure on Phillip to be more like his sister and let nature take its course.

I guess I am just letting myself get frustrated that things are not going as smoothly, and letting my first child's actions influence too greatly what my expectations of normalcy in the second should be. I'm being totally unfair. It's not as if he is doing anything out of the norm, it's just that everything from academics to emotional levels and even confidence issues aren't as easy for him.

How can it be that two children can have the same parents; grow up in the same house with the same environment and turn out to be so different? They don't even like the same foods or movies, he's totally messy and she's a neat freak, she's outgoing and good-natured and he's shy and sometimes a little moody, she's totally focused, always wanting things in order and he's a scatter brain constantly tearing things apart to see how they work.

Yet I hear this over and over again with other friends and family members. We all see this phenomenon being repeated throughout our world; we may all be created equally, but also we are all definitely created uniquely.

If we just step back and look at this for a minute we can appreciate the irony. Yet still, we are surprised by our children's differences even though we each have probably lived with this same experience in our own childhood families. How similar are we to our own siblings or our aunts and uncles for that matter? We could each point out various traits that are unique to each of us as well as traits in others which are comparable. Some attributes coming from Mom and others like Dad, even ones that are similar to an aunts or uncles, still others that are unlike anyone within our family circle.

I am fascinated and baffled by how our individual personalities, values and character traits are developed and the role we as parents play. Then consider the effect of what birth order one holds in the family, as that also seems to play an important part in personality development.

27

I can see how my own influence with my children helped mold the older sister (the responsible self-reliant one) and little brother (the more dependent needy one). It's also understandable that Stephanie adopted a lot of my ideals and habits just from the daily exposure. I can see where I expect her, being the older child, to behave more responsibly and independently than her little brother.

Yes, I can see now how I dealt an injustice to my son by the way I have treated him, always coddling him as the baby and, possibly not allowing him to grow up. I believe children typically conduct themselves according to expectations that are projected and expressed to them by parents.

We all know if you tell a child their stupid or ugly long enough they will believe it, if you tell a child they are smart or cute they will also take that to heart. Parents influence, attention and affirmation are immeasurable in shaping how a child thinks and feels about themselves.

What an incredible responsibility we all have as parents in the shaping of our future generations and we only get one shot at it. I find myself thinking I must do a better job helping Phillip grow into a more responsible young man. Maybe I should have raised my expectations a little higher for him from the beginning.

As Steph flies through the early years of her adolescence I feel an enormous pride in the confident, practical minded and thoughtful young lady that I can clearly see she will be one day. There is also the assurance I always feel in Steph's ability to make sound decisions and the trust I can put in her sense of responsibility.

Being so sure of her mind set, I therefore continued to turn the bulk of my attention to Phillip who I feel needs much more guidance. This is not to say that our heart to heart talks disappear, she is always eager to discuss any number of topics that come up in the news, school or what is going on in the lives of her many different friends.

This openness to learn about dealing with life is not exclusive to just me, she enjoys sitting around the kitchen table with me, her aunts, and Memaw as we discuss our daily trials. She always seems to be ready to listen and take to heart what her elders have to say.

As the summer arrives before Steph starts the ninth grade, we buy our first house in the Dallas suburbs. Starting in a new school is not new to Steph or Phillip, since both Mike and I have moved around the Dallas area fairly often, sometimes requiring a school change. I know changing schools can be hard on children, especially when they reach their teens, even though they both seem to make friends fairly easily. I am determined not to move again until they are both out of high school so they won't have to go through another disruption. We are all so excited about our new home and neighborhood.

The summer is passing quickly with us all settling into our fixer-upper home. As I pull into the drive after long days at work, I often find them both outside painting the faded siding on the house or in the yard planting flowers in our newly created garden. I smile as I realize they too have listened and learned from watching their Memaw and Papa's take charge kind of mindset. Smile that just maybe; I've passed on some of those things I have learned.

On days like these, memories of my childhood often come flooding back to me. This particular day brings a summer lesson to my mind.

There I am, about ten years old with my Daddy on the shore of the Lake Ouachita where we go camping every summer. Holding my fishing pole, I'm standing there pouting because he won't bait my hook for me. "Please Daddy. Just do it one more time for me" I plead. As he cast his line out, he smiles easily at me and replies, "I told you, not this year. If

29

you're going to be a fisherman, you have to learn to bait your own hook."

Frustrated that I can't change his mind, I sit down to just watch him. Daddy looks over at me and says, "You know there's not always going to be someone around to do everything for you. Beside, it feels better when you do things on your own."

As the afternoon sun beats down on us, I stubbornly sit there watching him enjoy himself. I'm angry that he won't give in, jealous because he seems to be having such a good time without me. After a while Daddy begins to gathers up his gear, "It's getting too hot, fish won't be biting now" he says.

"But I still want to fish" I tell him as I grab the box of worms. He smiles, pats me on the head and climbs the hill towards camp. Opening the lid, I select the fattest longest worm I can find. "I'll show him", I say to myself as I bite my lip and stick the hook through its body. "Eewwhh, this is so gross."

As I cast my line out into the lake, I feel a sense of satisfaction. Somehow all traces of my anger and jealously are gone. How long it took I don't know, but suddenly something hit my line almost making me drop my pole.

Remembering that Daddy always told me "you have to set the hook or you'll lose him" I pull up on my line and start to scream "Daddy, Daddy, I got one!" From the top of the hill Daddy calls to me as I struggle to turn the reel, "Are you sure it's not just a tree branch?"

"No, it's a fish, Daddy, I did it!" I scream as I ran up the hill, dragging my pole, line and the biggest fish any of us had caught all week. In shock, my Daddy just stands there, grinning at me and my accomplishment, as my large mouth bass flops on the shore.

I'm not sure if, at that age, I fully grasped the lesson I learned that day. All I remember is the pride I felt as we ate my catch that night and the look my Daddy passed my way. But now after years of similar childhood lessons, I understand the importance and the necessity of doing things for your self. All it often requires is taking a deep breath and just doing things that are sometimes unpleasant. The rewards of self reliance can be so fulfilling.

As my mind returns to my children, I smile again, as I realize both of them have become fearless and practical in tackling the numerous projects that our fixer upper home needs. Phillip defiantly is showing signs of inheriting Papa's mechanical ability to repair almost anything and Steph easily mimics her Memaws determination and organizational skills to the tee. Smile again, as I realize they are discovering, lessons learned and rewards received through difficulties and distasteful tasks are sometimes the most invaluable ones.

Before the end of summer we decide to take a vacation to Austin to see the state capital, then on to San Antonio for a short stay on the River Walk and visit Sea World. We are all very excited since this is the first real vacation we have really ever been able to afford. Not that it it's such a big deal like going to Hawaii or somewhere tropical but it's a start. We have such a blast and I decide with a new found determination to take them somewhere every year.

Fall progresses and so does my daughter. Steph quickly makes new friends and joins in several school activities. In spite of the move to a new neighborhood and being her first year of high school, she thrives in all classes. By the midterm her guidance counselor decides to move her into advance placement classes. English and writing especially come easy to her allowing her to show off her lovely script. Not surprisingly she finds that she really loves the childhood development courses she is taking and begins thinking about becoming an elementary school teacher.

31

I love the idea since she is so wonderful with children and enjoys babysitting so much. I know in my heart she will make a fabulous elementary school teacher as well as be very happy in that profession. Isn't that really all we want as parents, for our children to be happy in what they do?

On the other hand I have no idea what Phillip will do as an adult. I no longer hold out hope that his academic abilities will ever catch up to the level of his generous heart, sweet comical nature or his simple honest loyalty. But then those traits too, should make any parent just as proud.

Steph's relationships with her many friends shows sound judgment as all of them are kind, considerate, determined young men and women with similar desires to make their own way responsibly in the world.

One young lady in particular has become her best friend and is a mirror image of my daughter, intelligent, self motivated, sensible and kindhearted. They lean on, support and care for each other like sisters. I am beginning to no longer be the main support for Steph and it is leaving me with a huge vacant feeling.

With less attention needed at home I turn my focus to my work. Since the divorce, I have had a variety of jobs, a long distance operator which lead to a customer service rep at the same company. After leaving that company, I primarily pursued customer service type positions until several years ago when one of those positions also included assisting with some accounting duties. The more involved I was with that department the more I became interested in accounting work.

It's not that I have ever been that proficient in math, but discovered that not only did I enjoy the detailed processes but that I was also good at it. Good at organizing, researching and reconciling the puzzles that make up the whole accounting picture. I know it sounds boring to most people but I like tedious crapola, I enjoy turning a pile of chaos into an ordered wealth of information.

Recently, I accepted a new accounting position with the firm where I now work. Accepting this new type of position could turn out to be a new responsibility at just the wrong time, but then maybe it is just the right time. I will soon discover the truth to the thought that sometimes having a challenging distraction can be such a blessing.

Three years ago Daddy retired as a senior vice president from the same manufacturing company where he had worked for almost forty years. Just before his retirement my parents had bought land and built a new house in the country an hour and a half south of Dallas.

As the heat of the summer arrives I am given some heartbreaking news, my Daddy is diagnosed with advance stage lung and bone marrow cancer. With the cancer also attacking in a variety of other places, there is not much that can be done; needless to say, we are all an emotional mess.

As I try to learn new responsibilities at work and care for the house, while spending as much time as possible with my parents, Steph and Phillip quickly become my emotional support. They never complain about the long hours we spend there or the hours I spend on the phone with Mama, as I attempt to let her vent the pain and frustration that she tries to hide so well.

Now more than ever, our family motto becomes "just keep moving, keep putting one foot in front of the other." We also must never forget Mama's favorite phrase "this to shall pass". Though a part of us wants the little amount of time we have left, to never pass, as we desperately cling to the few moments we know we have left with him. But as the time passes and we watch Mama and Daddy each in their own separate suffering, we begin to silently hope it will pass soon.

Mama inspires us all with her steadfast strength and endurance as she cares for Daddy with love, patient tenderness and amazing fortitude in an effort to grant his wish of staying at home to the end. She makes sure we all fully

33

understand each and every symptom at each stage so we aren't surprised by anything. That's the way they have always handled situations as we were growing up and their openness in this crisis helps us to somewhat accept the rapid changes in Daddy.

Even though we were always aware of our parents love and devotion for each other, as the months pass we discover how precious their commitment to each other truly is. Seeing Mama doing everything possible to make sure Daddy is not only comfortable, but her efforts to enable him to enjoy as many moments with friends and family as he wants, shows us the real meaning of compassion and love. She never crumbles or falls apart in front of him even though I'm sure he knows she is dying inside right along with him.

I always thought of Daddy as a strong, proud, determined man but I never really considered the source of that view, it was just always there. This weekend as all our family gathered at my parents home, the source of this belief became all so clear to me. Standing in the kitchen watching Mama put the final touches on a salad, I comment to her, "Daddy looks to be in a lot of pain."

As she stretches the plastic wrap over the salad bowel, I notice her take a deep breath before she quietly replies, "Yes he is, but he won't take his morphine until everyone leaves." This baffles me, "But why?" I ask. As she looks toward the living room where Daddy is watching a ball game, Mama adds, "It makes him too dopey." As tears well up in her eyes she continues, "He just doesn't want to miss a minute." Then she squared her shoulders, took another deep breath and said "this too shall pass".

I witness this same phenomenon over and over again in the weeks that follow. Daddy exhibits his unparalleled strength and endurance, as I see him time and time again refuse his pain medication. Even now as we near the end, when he needs his dose of morphine so desperately, he will put it off as long as possible to be fully alert, so he can enjoy every moment possible with his loved ones.

I am amazed and yet comforted by his ability to talk frankly about his illness and emanate death, how he so easily shares his joys, his regrets in the life he has lived and in the remaining life he will miss out on. He has accepted his fate with a firm resolve and is only concerned that the woman he loves more than life itself will be okay after he is gone.

As communicating is becoming more and more difficult for him, Daddy seizes on what he knows is a fading opportunity. He takes each of his children aside several times to get assurance that we will make sure Mama will carry on with her own life, and find a new measure of happiness. Hearing him describe her as a vivacious woman needing companionship is a little more than any of us were expecting to hear. Though he doesn't seem at all embarrassed by the expression, vivacious, we are all taken aback; southern traditional children don't usually think of their mother in those terms.

One conversation I had with Daddy this past weekend, I have not yet shared with anyone as it was a very private moment between us. He spoke of his life and how he, a man with not even a high school diploma could rise from a simple dock worker to a senior vice president of a fairly large corporation through what most would accredit to his own hard work, determination and company loyalty. Yet, he attributed his success to something entirely different; solely to the strength and steadfast support of his wife, he believes that he would have achieved nothing without her standing firmly by his side.

After he let that sink in my mind for a moment, he went on to tell me how much I was like Mama. I had always been told I looked so much like my mother but never had I dreamed I could be like her in personality or character. Yet there I was, with Daddy telling me he saw her strength in me; asking me, for his sake, to stand by her side, to be strong for

35

her in the days after he was gone. He told me how important he thought it was for the ones we love, to have someone to be strong for them, to be their rock, so when they face those unbearable trials it would give them unimaginable strength to continue on.

I, being the overly emotional one in the family, the one who cries at the drop of a hat, thought it preposterous that I could ever be someone's strength, someone's rock. I couldn't even sit through those AT&T reach out and touch someone commercials shown on T.V. ten years ago or so, without bursting into tears. Yet, this was my father, a man that was rarely wrong about anything, asking me to promise to do this unthinkable thing for him and I could not deny him my promise.

As I said, I chose to not share this particular conversation with anyone but knowing Daddy, he may have very well had a similar talk with each of my siblings. What I do know, is that conversation changed something in me, and how I looked at myself. How I looked at what I could be, just because, my Daddy said so. Apparently a parent's influence never ceases.

With the weeks passing quickly, Daddy's health is slipping rapidly, and now he is at a point where he can barely speak, let alone participate in anything too physical. Yet being the proud man that he is, he still insists on getting out of bed and dressing every day. He does not want to be seen as a helpless bed ridden invalid nor does he want to miss out on anything going on in the rest of the house. He is determined to live each day as fully as possible.

Understand of course that most of the ten grandchildren are old enough to comprehend what is happening to their Papa, and cherish every minute they are able to spend with him. This naturally includes my own children who are now both in their early teens, and adore him very much. Their Papa has always been very playful and loving towards them, never failing to pay that special attention to each of them. I'm sure, just as his own children always felt, each of the grandchildren feel like they are his favorite and it is breaking all their hearts as they watch him deteriorate.

My daughter has become my support and comfort as I try my best to deal with what is happening to my parents. Regularly, as I end those nightly phone conversations, Steph comes into the kitchen to get the latest news on her Papa. I find myself being consoled and strengthened by her just as I had tried to do for Mama.

As I sit in the kitchen crying, Steph comes in and asks, "I heard you talking to Memaw, how's it going?" As my crying turns to heavy sobs, she leans over and hugs me and quietly says "Remember what Memaw always says, this too shall pass". Her arms around me are so comforting; slowly I begin to pull myself together. I take a deep breath and reply, "Yes, I remember … I just wish I knew what to do in the mean time". Steph gives me one of her radiant smiles and replies matter of factually, "You do like Memaw says, "Just keep putting one foot in front of the other".

It's amazing to me how comforting it is just hearing her say those words. It is heartwarming to realize she is paying such close attention to the value of those sentiments. I am thankful she will not fumble around for years as I did in my own youth before realizing the incredible strength one can draw from these words in times of crisis. So, that's what I do, I take a deep breath and go pull out the vacuum cleaner.

As the end for Daddy draws near, I find myself being pushed along the way by Steph in an effort to just keep me moving. Since I am physically, mentally and emotionally drained, I am thankful for the strength I am able to draw from her and the patience she shows me as I fumble through these last few weeks.

I know it sounds selfish of me to be counting on her for such support, yet these last few months, Steph has become someone I can rely on to express my frustration and sadness to. I don't feel like I can fall apart with Mama, since I am trying so hard to be strong for her. This is what I have always watched her do, and feel it is my duty to keep my promise to Daddy and be someone she can rely on. Still, I find it comforting to have such a support in Steph.

So I teeter back and forth between trying to be the rock and just being the scatter brain, not able to remember simple task such as putting shoes on before leaving for work or what year it is as I write checks out to pay the bills. Luckily both Steph and Phillip are able to laugh along with me at my inability to cook eatable meals forgetting to include crucial ingredients or the many times after going to the store for groceries I realize much too late that I have left them in the trunk for hours.

Sunday evenings are the most difficult since we spend the entire weekend with my parents at their house in the country. The drives home are mostly filled with tears and frustration as we discuss the obvious changes in their Papa, which not surprisingly often causes me to forget to take the correct turns, and we end up lost. All I can think about is Daddy's unbearable suffering, Mama's increasing grief, and how all our lives will forever be changed.

As a parent, I can't help but feel enormous guilt as I realize the last six months of my children's lives have been filled with grief over their Papa's illness, with little time for their own needs. They have never complained and often console me, telling me not to worry about them, but to just focus on Memaw and Papa.

With his wife and children standing by, Daddy passes away December 15th leaving us with such an unbelievable void. I have not yet found the time or inclination to buy a single Christmas present, nor have we put up our tree or any other decorations. My parents have always made such a big to-do over every holiday; it just seems too empty with out him to have any sort of celebration.

The funeral takes place on the 19th just before Christmas, but due to an extraordinarily amount of rain in the last month, we learn the morning of his service, that we are not able to bury him that day. As the six hundred capacity chapel fills to overflowing, in spite of another day of torrential rain, we sit with Mama in the Family Room.

"Olen would just hate this; ya'll know he doesn't like unfinished business," Mama says, struggling to hold back tears. "The director says we have to put him in one of those awful crypts until it dries up next week" she continues. My heart sinks to a new low as I visualize us all, having to go through separate graveside services after Christmas.

Looking into the chapel, my heart is pinched with grief as well as pride as I clearly see the evidence of the kind of man Daddy truly was. There is not one empty seat, aisles and the back foyer is packed, as people whose lives were touch by this man, jockey to find a place to pay they're respects. Long after the services, the chapel is still full of his friends, most of them I have known my entire life, sharing with us their personal stories of what Daddy meant to them.

The power of Words, words that are spoken with an abundance of love and respect again become a source of strength and comfort in a time when it is needed so much. It seems my world is becoming surrounded by the support of this particular power and it's a power greater than I ever imagined. More comforting than I can express.

So Christmas and New Years comes and goes without fan fair, as we each in our own way wrestle to continue on, while feeling so robbed of such an important figure in all our lives. Mama continues to be an inspiration to us all; showing great strength and determination to do as she always advised others to do, "to keep putting one foot in front of the other". Just as Daddy had warned, she puts on a brave face and insists that she is fine. We all continue to visit every weekend at first, and then gradually consult each other to assure that someone is visiting each weekend.

39

During the week, the nightly phone calls continue with Mama giving us reassurances that she is fine, though we all know better. She is more than adapt at putting on a brave face. You don't lose a love like they had, without having your heart ripped out and we know, all we can do is be there for her to lean on.

It seems to me, that all our children can learn so much from watching the important adults in their life and how they handle difficult situations. The examples we give them can become instruction books, guiding them as they face their own challenges, just as we may have learned from our elders. I feel I was fortunate to have what I consider several stellar role models growing up, always demonstrating strength, courage, compassion and determination. I only regret that it has taken me many years, to really appreciate the impact of their influence.

All of us can all look back through our lives and find people who made great impacts on us just by the way they behaved. We seem to be instinctively a species of observers, learning continually through the actions of others. I think it would benefit our society greatly if we all took more to heart, the impact we can have influencing the hundreds of people we come in contact with. Any one of us can remember a time when we were at a store, restaurant or mall and observed a behavior that we were either impressed by or repulsed by. I believe even these small impressions can contribute to shape our values and character in many different ways.

This belief makes me thankful that my children have such wonderful grandparents and believe they learned so much from watching them throughout the years. Steph is showing many signs of becoming a great example for future children as well. Her strength, fortitude and insight to life's trials are now called upon by her numerous friends as they face adolescence and she meets each occurrence with thoughtfulness and compassion.

We have been through so much in this past year. It feels like I have been walking through a thick fog and now suddenly I notice my daughter appears to have lost weight. I have been vaguely aware that she has not been eating well and complaining of stomach aches. This is understandable to me since Steph has walked every step of the last year with me and has been also grieving for her Papa. Add that to the strain of adolescence, starting in a new high school and living in a new neighborhood, I feel that it is most likely her nerves. A doctor's appointment agrees with my feelings and a nervous stomach diagnosis is given that she most likely will out grow as she matures and learns to cope with life's trials.

Nothing in Steph's attitude or nature has changed and her school work surprisingly is not suffering so I try not to be too concerned. Chalking it up to her being a bit of a worry wart like me, I make a mental note to keep an eye on her weight. I think most likely she is putting too much stress on herself, always being the determined, self disciplined perfectionist. However in her independent way she says, "Mom, your fussing over nothing, don't worry, I'm fine."

With the arrival of spring, Steph turns fifteen and as promised I enroll her in a summer driver's education school near our home. I always felt that it was important to allow her to get her beginner's permit as soon as possible so; she would have almost a year to practice with me before turning keys to a car over to her. I have to admit; now that that day has arrived I find it scary and nerve racking riding along with her.

After the first few times though she quickly puts my mind at ease as she pays such close attention to her surroundings and seems to have good judgment with distances. As I relax and let her drive more often, she quickly becomes confident and sure of her own abilities.

The first boyfriend arrives and as you can imagine, I worry; not due to any strange behavior on his or her part but just because that's what parents are suppose to do. He's a nice boy with good manners and seems to treat Steph well.

They spend a lot of time together and since he has his license and a car, I often find myself standing in the doorway waving goodbye to them. As all parents do, I can only hope I have instilled in her enough self respect for her to not tolerate any disrespect. I only want her to be happy and we all know it takes a lot more than a cute face and cool car to bring joy into a relationship.

With summer fast approaching she finds me on the back porch one Saturday as I'm drinking my morning coffee and says, "Hey Mom, I want to get a job for the summer". Hesitantly I answer, "A job, how are you going to get to and from work?" But she's way ahead of me, "I've already solved that, but this restaurant manager says I need your permission," as she whips out a piece of paper. As I struggle to keep up with Steph and her plans, all that comes to my mind is, who am I, that I should stand, in Miss Independent's way.

So with the arranged rides from friends who take her and pick her up, Steph begins her new job with one of her girlfriends at a steak house as a hostess. I think it will be good for her and might even keep her mind distracted from worries; maybe it will also help alleviate her stomach troubles.

Since her last visit to the doctor she has missed several days of school and has had to come home from school a few times. She is not able to eat much without getting cramps and continues to have diarrhea alternating with constipation. "Steph, honey, I think another trip to the doctor is in order" I say. She replies, "You're probably right, I'll, make an appointment".

Once again the doctor believes it is still due to her nerves but this time gives her some medicine to take to help settle her stomach. As she tells me "He told me to stay away from spicy and fatty foods" I have to laugh. No one has a healthier or sparser diet than Steph. "Well maybe you should

42

leave out the low fat yogurt." I tease, knowing that along with oatmeal that is pretty much all she consumes.

It seems my two children have learned the best time to approach me about something important to them is when I'm on the back porch drinking my Saturday morning coffee. Again Steph comes to me and asks, "Hey Mom, will you sign off on this? I found out that if I take summer classes, I can either graduate early or take college courses during my senior year."

I don't know why I still continue to be amazed by her; it seems she hasn't needed me for anything in a very long time. "Sure honey, why not?" I reply to her radiant smile. I am thrilled that she is taking her education so seriously. It's nice not having to push Steph in her pursuit of education, as I do my son, in his academic efforts. I know in my heart, I will never have to worry about her future as I do with Phillip, who continues to struggle in school.

CHAPTER 4   Summer 1996

Just before the new school year begins we take a five day trip to Cancun Mexico. I had saved all year and paid in advance for the all inclusive trip, then set money aside for the extra activities we wanted to do. Steph and I are packed days in advance; Phillip of course waits until the night before to think about it. Why am I surprised that we have to stay up late doing his laundry and getting him packed.

On the second day we go on a submarine ride to see a wide variety of spectacular fish and remarkable underwater reefs. We are having such a good time that is until I get violently sick as we rise back to the surface. I am thoroughly embarrassed as I rely on Steph to fill in as mom, to get us back to the hotel. I have to laugh at myself as I realize, she always seems to be able to hold me up in my time of need. Guilt pours over me as I remember how she must be feeling with her stomach flaring up with all the strange local food we are eating.

The next evening we arrive at the dock to go on a Pirate Dinner Party Boat with crazy pirates and wenches running amuck all over the boat as they serve us dinner. Needless to say, Phillip has selected the silliest trip imaginable, but it proves to be fun for all of us.

All during dinner I notice Steph again is not eating. I ask, "Are you okay, Honey?" Steph just replies "I just feel sick my stomach, but I'll be fine." This is becoming a constant message to me as I watch her pick at her food at most mealtimes and spend more than normal amount of time in the restroom.

The last activity we have scheduled is to go Jet Skiing and Parasailing. None of us has ever been on a Jet Ski so we rent two of them. Since Phillip is under fifteen we are told he can't drive. I, being the upstanding person that I am, after going out a ways from the rental site, allow Phillip to take over. Probably not such a bright idea, but what the heck, it's well worth the smile on his face. Besides he seems much more adapt at driving these blasted things than I am, which only adds to our fun.

Later in the day Steph and I quickly develop a love/hate feeling for Parasailing. I'm sure the worker's of the boat will be talking about the fearless mother/daughter team for months. This contraption is not the typical harness type ride but a bench ride with only a bar holding us in the seat.

As the wind sways us in our seat all the way up and down, we can't help but laugh and scream the entire time as we nearly claw each other to death. We can't seem to agree on who was trying to protect who in our attempts to hold on to each other. It will take weeks for the scratches on our arms and legs to heal. As beautiful as it was, I can't imagine that we will ever do that again.

So the next school year begins with us refreshed and tan, ready to take on the daily hum drum once again. Much of the first semester is going as usual, with worries over my son's grades, while my daughter continues to excel in everything except the ability to digest her food properly. Steph continues to miss classes from time to time and I can't help notice her weight has dropped even more. So again, we return to the doctor, this time insisting he run some test to see if we can get a better idea of what's going on with her stomach.

Over the next few months she goes through a number of blood test as well as X-ray's, CAT scans and an upper G.I to see if they can find out what's causing her problem. The final diagnosis is termed as Irritable Bowel Syndrome, a condition I'm told is difficult to treat and greatly depends on a person's diet. Well that helps; she hardly eats anything anymore for fear that it will upset her stomach and has often resorted to suppositories to relieve her constipation.

So we take the information the doctor gives us home in hope that we can find the happy medium to her diet and at least we are assured Steph doesn't have anything fatal. Not surprisingly, now that my son is never ill, my daughter takes up the slack. Isn't it exasperating how there is always something for a parent to worry about.

I think it's important to trust that you've done a good job, step back a little and let them make more of their own choices. Mama often says both parent and child would survive adolescence better if, parents could be put to sleep when their child turns thirteen and not woke up until they turned twenty five.

I am beginning to see her reasoning in this, considering that most of the trials with teens are the internal worries a parent suffers through. And as I suffer, I find myself stressing them out right along with me with my nitpicking. I don't' think I'm very good at just sitting back and waiting for the other shoe to drop.

Steph and her boyfriend still appear to be getting along fine, still spending a lot of time together; sometimes at our house other times at his family home. I can't say for sure what goes on between them since this is one topic she rarely talks to me about. Yes, we continue to enjoy our talks about other things, but the topic of boyfriends seems to be off-limits for me.

I'm glad she still has her best friend to talk to, and I know she is a very level headed young lady who won't let her stand for any mistreatment. I'm not even sure why I worry;

47

he still seems like such a nice young man. I know, I know, I'm just a worry wart at heart.

Spring arrives with my daughter's sixteenth birthday and as planned, Steph gets her driver's license. And to think, I thought buying her first bra was an emotional crisis, but this is an entirely different ballgame. Though I am thrilled for her, I know in my heart she will drive off, in the not so new car I just bought her and rarely look back.

That's just her nature, to be independent and self-sufficient. How could I have not been more prepared for the feelings of loss I'm experiencing? Where did all those years go?

As parents, we go through continual changes in our roles as our children grow through adolescence. We must still be the protector, provider and teacher, but now in addition to these, we now must learn how to be the silent observer. We've taught them right from wrong, impressed upon them our values, guided and directed them for years. Now we arrive at this moment in their lives, where we must now just sit back and trust in our abilities as parents and them as young adults.

This driving force we have put into action over the years to shape them into productive adults, must now be curbed in their need to be more independent. Often it's much easier said than done; to let them go off and make their own mistakes when we have been there, done that and surely we know better. But isn't that the best way to learn; by trial and error? I find this to be a much greater struggle for me than I imagined, maybe this is also a trial and error period for me too.

Steph's responsible behavior with her new found independence is giving me the sense that she must have taken very detailed notes during all those childhood lessons. I'm finding that I never have to concern myself with the choices or decisions she makes; it seems she just always knows the right thing to do. Not surprisingly, she rarely needs me to make decisions and even though we still enjoy our close talks. I struggle as I discover myself in a reduced role in her life. I've felt like the center of her world for so long and now I must resign my post, at least partially, and let her soar toward new skies.

I have always felt it is my responsibility as a parent to teach my children as they transition into adulthood to learn how to manage their money. I don't think it is fair to thrust them out into the world without trying to teach them to live within their means. As hard as it is for me to do just that myself, I know their financial future will also depend on it.

One of the agreements I had years before she was able to drive was, when she got her license, I would get her a car but, she would pay for her own insurance and gas. Now Steph comes to me and says "Mom, I want my own phone." Not seeing this as such a bad idea I tell her, "Okay, I'll pay to have it installed, but you make the monthly payment, deal?" The glare from her smile almost blinds me. "Hey, I want a phone too." Phillip complains.

As I stand there with perplexity on my face, Steph chucks him on the shoulder and says, "You can use mine, Brother, until your old enough to work; just don't give out the number to everybody you know, oh and no calls after ten, deal?" There, problem solved, how does she always do that, more importantly why? Looking at the two of them, standing there together, smiling at each other, I have no choice but to just smile right along with them.

All Steph's bills she pay's without fail every month, as well as buying a lot of her own clothes. She is very good with her self imposed budget and soon wants her own checking account. I see no problem with trusting her with this, since getting her drivers license she often has my debit card to buy groceries for me and has proven to be very careful with money. We both are very proud as we leave the bank with her new account and check register in tow.

During the next year, Steph breaks up with her boyfriend. I am given no explanation except for her to say she hasn't been happy with him. I tell her, "I always hoped you would date other boys, I think it's important to see all your choices. Dating is like finding your favorite ice cream; you should to try many flavors to see which one is your favorite. Sure you may like several but; this way you can find the one special flavor that's the most enjoyable for you."

Laughing at my silly analogy, she simply replies, "Where do you come up with these things, Mom?" I know it sounds silly but I often use these types of comparisons to get her to think about the lessons in life we all need to understand. Maybe I over use these types of lessons a little too much but I can't seem to stop myself.

On a more personal note, I'm so excited, nervous, but still very excited. The Financial Analyst/Office Manager, Colleen, at the engineering firm where I work has turned in her three week notice and recommended me for the position. Well, the title is a bit of a stretch, it's really more of a staff accountant position who also runs the administrative department. But the owners, who offered the position to me, like fancy titles and I must admit I tend to like the ego boost it provides.

Colleen has been training me for the past few months in what I knew to be some of her duties. I thought it was just for the purpose of filling in for her when she is on vacation or so I can help her out from time to time. Now I know, it was for very different reasons, reasons which make me proud and a little scared all at the same time.

I don't think managing eight or nine employees will be a problem for me. I've had some experience managing two or three people to some extent already without the title. I watched Daddy manage people all my life and learned a lot from him over the years. I remember him telling me once, "Managing is not only about delegating duties but most importantly, how you ask them to do those duties. Treat each person with great respect and appreciation and you'll find yourself getting a lot more done".

Though I don't have a degree in accounting and only have had five years of accounting experience, I know I can do what will be required of me. I addition to performing the typical office manager duties, I will be overseeing and managing budgets, bank accounts, collections and preparing reports on the monthly financial status of the company. I have done each of these duties myself at one time or another in the last few years. The difference is now I will be responsible for all of these areas together.

Thankfully, Colleen has offered to give me guidance for the next few months over the phone if I need it and most likely, I will. I guess I will just have to rely on what Mama always says, "It can't be that hard", "Just keep putting one foot in front of the other".

Steph continues to be involved in the child development program at school and is determined to be an early education school teacher helping to shape the minds of America's next generation. Children have always been drawn to her for attention which she thoroughly enjoys giving them with inexhaustible patience and animated energetic playfulness. Her understanding of the workings of their minds and emotional needs is complemented by her creative ability to spark their interest in anything she suggests.

Winter arrives with complaints of stiff aching joints in Steph's fingers, hip and knees. She describes it as a burning dull pain that makes her joints feel rigid. Her only relief comes from running hot water over them and the use of a heating pad. After a trip to the doctor we discover she has bursitis and the beginnings of arthritis in those joints.

These problems run heavily in my family, myself included, however no one has ever had these symptoms this early in their life. Steph takes the news all in stride with her usual attitude and mind set. "Well it figures, I'm guess I'm just turning into a medical mystery." she says with a smile, making light of the situation. Sympathetically, I wonder and worry just what her future joints have in store for her.

Tired of her hostess job at the steak house, Steph decides to take a position in a clothing store at the mall. She wants to work more hours—and then there's the added bonus of getting a discount on the latest teen clothes they sell. She continues to pay all her own bills, manage her money and checkbook well. She never asks me for anything, choosing instead to purchase what she needs or wants herself. Often she surprises Phillip and I with thoughtful presents she sees at the mall and thinks we will like. It's nice, though knowing her as we do, her kindness really doesn't surprise us.

Somewhere during the next year Steph's stomach troubles seem to miraculously improve as she puts on some weight. Maybe, the first diagnosis of nervous stomach was correct and she has worked her way through it resolving on her own the apprehension that comes with growing up. Sure her joints still bother her, mostly during a big change in the weather, but she is learning to cope with that as well and rarely complains.

As spring arrives, I begin dating a man, Matt, that I meet at work. In fact he was one of the first people I had to interview when I became the office manager this past year. After observing his work ethic for almost a year now, I find him to be an intelligent, funny and hard working man with a spontaneous attitude about life. Not to mention tall, dark and handsome, but I think the spontaneous part is what attracts me most.

Being the kind of person who schedules what days she dust, vacuums and cleans the toilets; I think I have a need for an influence in my life that can persuade me to loosen up a little. You know, take the road less traveled a time or two - live on the wild side – maybe just a little.

I find that I like everything in my life to fit into a tidy little box and I'm not so sure that's healthy. I don't mean that I'm one of those obsessive people, who have everything labeled in neat little rows in the cabinets facing all exactly the same direction.

But I also can see how my orderly influence has leaked over onto Steph and she does have a label maker, and a day planner, and antiseptic wipes and a bulletin board for her schedule and ....well, you get my drift. Anyway Matt and I have only been out a few times, but so far so good.

Anyway with her organizational skills and dedication to details, I believe that's a big part of why Steph persistently does so well in school. But with her also dating several different young men and participating in so many activities, I can't fathom how she finds the time for it all. She is always so full of energy and life, with such a positive perspective it often keeps me in amazement.

Steph has become such a beautiful, vibrant, and delightful young lady with the world at her feet, ready to take on any challenge. I am so proud of her, for all she had become and what I can see her accomplishing with that determined steadfast resourceful mind of hers. She continues to amaze me. A mother could not be more pleased than I, with who their child has become.

It's a beautiful Saturday during the summer before Steph's senior year and I arrive home from an afternoon date with Matt, to find that she had been rushed to the hospital. "What happened, are you alright?" I ask. "I'm fine," Steph replies as she gingerly sits down on the couch. "At lunch I went upstairs to the food court get a bite to eat."

As she held her hand up to stop my questions she continues, "On my way up the escalator, there was this elderly lady in front of me, she tripped and fell back into me. When I tried to catch her, I lost my balance and fell all the way down to the bottom."

Her lack of usual cheerful animation concerns me. With growing unease over her change in demeanor, I bite my tongue as she slowly drags out the rest of the story. "I bumped my head and the security department called an ambulance. I felt fine but they said I seemed disoriented. The paramedics made me go to the hospital to get checked out."

As I feel the back of her head, finding the goose egg bump I ask, "What did the doctor say? Are you sure you're okay?" Grimacing at the touch, Steph replies "they ran a few test, said I have a concussion and just to see my doctor by the end of the week." "The worse thing was they wouldn't let me leave without an adult. I had to call Dad" she says wrinkling up her nose. Puzzled by why that's such a bad thing, I reply, "Now Steph, that couldn't be so bad, I'm glad you were able to get a hold of him."

"You need a cell phone, Mom, will you get one now?" she pleads asked. Sitting there next to her, seeing her so out of character, so childlike, pains me. I felt like a parental failure for not being there for her in one of the few times that she needed me. My lack of a cell phone had come up many times before; stubbornly I just really didn't see the need, that is, before today. "Okay, Honey, your right, I should get one."

Throughout the rest of the evening Steph assures me, other than a headache, she feels okay. With the promise of a cell phone in her grasp, she begins to tease me for being so stubborn about not wanting one of those new fangled things. Seeming more her self now, in her playful way she pokes fun at me, saying I don't really care about her as much as my new interest in Matt. I know she is making light of the situation by pretending to be a cry baby, something she never has been. It feels good to laugh a bit about things, now that the scare is past.

We all have moments while raising our children where we feel like kicking ourselves for not being there or not doing something that we later felt like we should have done. It's only natural to sometimes second guess our actions or re-evaluate the decision we have made when it regards the most precious people in our lives.

The ever present Mama Bear in us is always striving to protect, nurture and guide those in our charge. And so even after Steph's reassurances, I continue to feel guilty for letting my guard down and not being there for her.

Steph continues to date several different young men and now for some reason feels she can talk more to me about them and how they behave. It's comforting to know she quickly move on to the next courtier if they turn out to be unacceptable to her. "I don't mean to be too picky Mom, I just don't see the point in wasting time with guys I don't feel right about." she says. "Oh honey, don't look at it as being picky or not, just think about it as needing to find the right one for you" I replied. I am so glad she has enough confidence in herself to know she deserves to find the best match for her.

It's the end of summer and I have saved and planned our vacation for months, five days to the Cayman Islands. With Steph and Phillip rapidly approaching adulthood, I realize that there will not be many more opportunities for family trips. We pack our bags days in advance, well Steph and I do anyway, once again, we stay up late washing and packing Phillips clothes. "I'm sorry, I'm sorry," Phillip keeps saying. "Don't worry Brother, it's no big deal" replies Steph.

Thinking to my self, "Sure no big deal, our plane leaves at seven thirty in the morning, we're an hour away from the airport and we only have to be there an hour and a half before the flight. We might as well not go to bed at all." As I take a deep breath, I hear Mama whisper softly in my ear "it could be worse; you could not be going at all". "Okay, okay." I silently reply.

Our hotel is right on the beach with spectacular views displaying the whitest sand I have ever seen. We purchase only two excursions this time and excitedly we walk across the street to a jeep rental center with the idea in mind that we explore the island on our own. "Uhh Mom, they drive on the wrong side of the road here, are you sure you can you do that?" questions Phillip. "It can't be that hard" I reply, trying to hide the apprehension that's creeping into my mind. Looking over to Steph, I get a reassuring smile and boldly stride into their office.

Before getting into the jeep, Phillip insists on taking the canvas roof and side coverings off, "this is going to be so cool" he beams, climbing into the front seat. As I fight to retain control over my nerves, I pull out onto the street. "Left side Mom, left side", Steph continually reminds me, as we search for adventure amidst a sea turtle farm and several remote beaches.

Phillip, looking over the site seeing brochure picked up at the rental center, suddenly shouts, "I want to go to Hell". Astonished at his free use of a word that's not typically heard in our home, I cry out "What did you say"? With a satisfying grin on his face Phillip continues, "It's not a curse word, see," pointing at the brochure, "it's a City called Hell, I want to go to Hell, it will be fun going to Hell. Steph wants to go to Hell too, don't you Steph, don't you want to go to Hell"? As I turn the jeep towards Hell City, Steph and I crack up laughing at his clever silliness.

As often happens every afternoon in the late summer tropics, a torrential rain suddenly soaks us a few hours later in our uncovered jeep. "Do you still think this is really so cool, Brother?" teases Steph while attempting to use one of the side window coverings to shield herself and me from the rain. As Phillip reaches past her to grab a covering, he quips back at her, "Yes, we needed to be cooled off, it was hot in Hell". Laughter fills the air as Steph calmly reminds, "Left side Mom, left side".

The next morning sun is shining brightly as we arrive for our first excursion, to snorkel and conch shell dive.

Snorkeling is fun once I get use to it but after seeing a Barracuda, Steph and I decide to get back in the boat.

Moving to the dive area, the Captain of the boat tells us "the conch shells are down about twenty feet, so you will need to take your life jacket off in order to dive that deep." Glancing over at Steph, I see my own dread reflecting back at me through her eyes. Neither of us really likes getting our face wet and we certainly don't consider ourselves good swimmers.

"No problem, I'll get them Mom," Phillip declares as he tosses his life jacket aside and leaps over the side of the boat. Steph and I smile as we peer over the side watching our fish impersonator dive deeper and deeper into the water. Once, twice, then rising to the surface the third time, Phillip beams with pride as the entire group breaks out in cheers. The crew shows how impressed they are by serving him, the first bowl of fresh conch stew. Though I have to admit I am a little jealous of his abilities, Steph and I thank him for saving the day.

The day before we leave for home, we wake up early and rush to get ready for our final excursion. "Mom, I have a really bad headache. Can I just stay in our room" whispers Steph. Worries have slowly grown in the last few weeks over this repeated scenario. I asked "What, another one?", as I reach out to gently rub her head. Steph backs away saying, "yeah, but I'll be fine, I just need quiet". Not wanting to leave her alone "But you can't miss the sting-rays, this was your idea, maybe we should all skip it." I reply.

Seeing a look of disappointment on his face, Steph replies, "You have to take Phillip, I'll feel worse if I'm the reason he misses swimming with sting-rays, please Mom, I'll be fine." My mind is torn, I don't want to leave Steph nor do I want Phillip to miss a once in a lifetime experience. "Just take some pictures for me, really, go, I'll be fine." urges Steph.

57

"Okay, but when we get back home, you need to see the doctor again" I say as I hesitantly finish getting ready to leave. Grabbing my purse we reluctantly hurry to catch our boat. An hour later we arrive at the sandbar and are given instructions to not make any sudden movements when we are in the water with the sting-rays. Phillip's adventurous spirit pulls me along with him out onto the sandbar and we are suddenly surrounded by dozens of sting-rays.

As I relax in the waist deep water, they rub against my legs, turning and winding their way around me, over and over. With their large eyes staring up at me, skin so soft, I get the overwhelming feeling that the sting-rays are very much like animated kitty cats.

I snap picture after picture as the crew shows Phillip how to feed them and pick them up. Though sad that Steph is missing this adventure, the grin on Phillip's face soothes me. We both have a fabulous time, a time I'm sure I will remember with tender fondness, for years to come.

Summer is over and senior year begins with a frenzy of activities ranging from portraits to ring and gown fittings, senior luncheons, invitation printing and let's not forget "The Prom." When did graduating become such an enormous expense and drama? I do agree, it should be celebrated and acknowledged with pride. But sometimes I wonder if we are setting our children up for great disappointments later in life, for just doing their job. Thankfully, most seniors have taken enough credits in prior years, so they almost have time to participate in all the activities scheduled during this mad rush to graduate.

Ever since the escalator accident, Steph's headaches have continued. I insist she return to our family doctor and because of the accident this past summer, he refers her to a neurologist. The first appointment she goes on her own, but when he suggests a MRI and CAT scan she ask me to meet her there. Now that she is having blinding headaches at least once a week, we realize we are both more worried than we wanted to admit.

Our main concern is possible damage to her brain caused by the escalator accident that may have gone undetected. I have spent many nights, lying awake, worrying about my little girl and her recent sufferings. Nothing we have tried, aspirin, Tylenol, Advil, Excedrin or any over the counter pain relief has given her any form of relief from these headaches.

All she can do is go to bed with the lights out, blinds drawn and be still in total silence. Even this only allows her to tolerate the pain but never gives her the relief she so desperately needs. I can see in her face the minute one of them is coming on, her eyes give it away. Always the trooper, she tries to shrug it off, she never wants me or anyone to worry too much about her.

With all of the tests completed, the neurologist calls us to come into the office for the results. Trying to understand his medical terminology is so confusing, and seeing the total look of bewilderment in our eyes, he changes his vocabulary to more layman's terms.

He assures us that for one, the accident hasn't caused any permanent damage and that Steph's brain functions appear to be perfectly normal. The test show no swelling or blockages that give him reason for the concern. "So why" I ask, "is she having such fierce headaches then"? He explains that he believes what she is experiencing is migraines or cluster headaches.

Well, it's a relief to know that there isn't a tumor growing or an aneurysm about to explode. He explains that although there isn't a cure, he can try several medications to see if they help give her a little relief. Thinking to myself "a little relief is the best we can hope for?" That's not very encouraging. One of the newly developed medications he feels can be the most helpful is Imitrex, which is administered as an injection. We decide to give it a try and he gives us a few samples along with instructions on how to use them.

The neurologist suggests therapy with a psychologist to help deal with any stress that may be triggering her headaches. Steph interrupts, "I don't want to spill my guts to some stranger. I wouldn't be stressed out if I didn't have the headaches", "besides if I need to talk I can talk to Mom". I've never been to a therapist but if the doctor thinks it will help, I'll go along with the idea. I convince Steph to try it for a while and see if there is any noticeable improvement. So we take the recommended list of professionals in our area and make an appointment with one of them for her first visit.

It isn't long before we have the opportunity to test out the new drug the neurologist had given her. At first, we debate over who is going to stick her in the leg. The injection device isn't a needle and syringe but a stick pen device that actually looks like a fat pen. When you firmly tap your skin, a tiny needle pops out, piercing the skin with the medicine in it.

I'm not typically squeamish about such things, nor is Steph, but the idea of hurting her to give her relief, sends a stab of pain to my heart that I had not anticipated. Mix this with my daughter's notion of someone sticking her in the leg on purpose, gives us an unforeseen dilemma. In the end, it is my determined courageous little girl who braves the deed and sticks herself with the contraption. I'm not at all sure whose relief she is thinking of more, hers or mine.

Well, the verdict is in, the headache is relieved slightly; however the side effects she experiences are more bothersome than the headache. "It makes me feel funny, disoriented somehow and I'm dizzy. My arms are tingling," she says as she rushes to the bathroom to vomit.

It wasn't long until the headache returns more intensely than ever. With disappointment and frustration I put Steph to bed, turn out the lights and rub her head for a while. As I leave her room I feel overwhelmingly disheartened and helpless, thinking that my little girl, after a childhood of virtually no illnesses, is turning into a medical mystery.

As with Steph, I had enrolled Phillip in driving school after he turned fifteen and now that he is sixteen he has his driver's license and a used car. He's a surprisingly careful driver and quickly finds a job delivering pizzas' after school. He's thrilled that they allow him to have all the pizza and subs he wants and often brings home treats for us. He continually finds ways to remind me that life often is, just about the little things.

He has always had a generous nature and this wonderful trait continues even more so, now that he has his own money. This sometimes is a problem for me though, since he often treats friends to movies or other things and then doesn't have money for his car insurance or gas. As usual I coddle him, not wanting to make him feel bad. But I'm beginning to see that I am reinforcing the process of not letting him grow up and learn responsibility.

What is it about me that allow me to teach responsibility to one child, and then apparently deny those lessons to the next child? If I believe my influence has something to do with Steph being so responsible, then I must also accept that I am influencing Phillip to be irresponsible. With the arrival of Matt into our lives and his frankly spoken observations, I am beginning to recognize the disservice I am dealing to my son. But, old habits - die hard.

Throughout the fall, Steph's headaches increase in frequency and duration. So we do what most people do in this modern age; we turn to the internet. We go in search of answers to what may be causing these headaches as well as what other's do as remedies. We find a wide variety of ideas and antidotes, that really only lead to more questions, so naturally we decide to try some. What we discover over the next few months is that no matter what she does, the headaches come and go with a will of their own, whenever they chose.

61

I learn an enormous amount about the last frontier, our brain, and how it is believed to work. It's such an amazing and complicated part of our bodies that will provide a never ending supply for research studies in the decades to come. Each year the medical profession discovers new avenues of research in the causes of this most debilitating problem. Hopefully many advances will be realized in the treatment and prevention for those suffering with migraines. This entire process has taught me a valuable lesson; the need to play a very active role in understanding our afflictions if, for no other reason than to help doctors to treat us more effectively.

When Steph first began having this problem, I read many different articles and books, which most were all difficult for a non-medical person to read and understand. Recently though, I found a site to be especially helpful in understanding the brain (in real people language) and it is well worth the time to read. If you're interested in getting a good explanation about how our mind works, check out the website below.

TRAUMATIC BRAIN INJURY SURVIVAL GUIDE By Dr. Glen Johnson,Clinical Neuropsychologist-Website @ www. tbguide. com

Mama continually emphasizes that the more we understand about any given situation the better we are able to deal with it. Some people prefer to take the ostrich approach about things, you know, what you don't know won't hurt you; but Mama strongly believes in the power of knowledge. It seems to me, being open to and having a thirst for new ideas and information is how we have grown from cave man to our current brilliant selves.

I have to admit; sometimes in my desperation to "fix the problem of her headaches" it's possible that I go over board sometimes in my search and suggestions. From time to time Steph becomes a little annoyed with me for my over eager helpfulness. This is a new conflict for us and I struggle with stepping back so as not to stress her even more. Sometimes it's just too hard to put the Momma Bear to sleep.

Though Steph has been going to therapy for months, I think it's still too early to tell if the sessions are doing any good. And even though she still isn't thrilled about going, I convince her to give it some more time. It's been six months since the start of these headaches and nothing we have tried has improved them. It seems all she can do is ride them out.

So with an attitude that could make NFL players across the nation, step back and take notice, my determined little girl decides that her headaches are apparently something she is just going to have to learn to live with. Along with her other ailments, Steph decides she will just have to do her best to ignore them and get on with her life. I conclude I'm just going to have to get accustom to being amazed by her determination.

My own life continues to improve at work and a growing relationship with Matt whom I have come to adore. We get along so well, we think alike in conservative political and economic terms, both have a rather silly sense of humor at times. Most importantly, I can talk to him about anything and everything. Matt's spontaneity continues to inspire me to loosen up my rigid need to plan everything, though sometimes I think he goes a little overboard with last minute changes. The struggle to keep my aggravation over this difference between us may become an issue, but being such a minor one, I think it is worth us working through the irritation.

Matt and I have become very close since we began dating eight months ago. And we decide to do what most people crazy about each other yet who have been married before do; we decide to live together for a while. While dating, Matt and I have not spent very much time at my home or with Steph and Phillip. They don't know each other that well and though I want to proceed with our plan, I realize that this may make the transition a little more difficult. So, throwing caution to the wind, Matt moves into our house mid-spring and we all begin to make the adjustment.

"The Prom"; need I say more? What an event this has turned into with the dresses, shoes, and boutonnieres and somewhere along the way every young lady that is to attend must get her nails, makeup and hair done by a professional. Don't think the guys have it any easier with their part, which includes the tux rental, dinner out, limo and now it apparently isn't enough to give a corsage but you need to bring a presentation bouquet as well. I don't know how they or their parents handle the stress and frenzy, much less the expense, as for me and Steph it is quite a strain.

The day of the prom arrives and Steph is a nervous wreck, with nail and hair appointments to go to, after working a short morning schedule at the mall. With work done, she is on her way to the appointments and her car stalls in the middle of a busy intersection. She frantically gets her car into a parking lot with the help of two very nice men, and then runs to find a pay phone. She calls us at home crying, upset about her car, the appointments she may miss and how she won't have time now to pick up her dates' boutonnière before the flower store closes.

Matt and I race to the rescue to the location she gives us and I see she's in a scattered panic. "This is so unlike her." I mention to Matt, "She is usually so composed about hectic schedules or disastrous mishaps." I'm taken aback a little bit and get caught up in her frustration.

Thankfully, Matt sees what needs to be done and does what he's best at; He cuts to the chase in his first family crisis and delegates the needed duties with firm resolve. His take charge attitude quickly calms the situation and we all are disbursed to our given assignments. We leave Matt standing in the parking lot next to her car and as I drop Steph off at her first appointment, I find myself wondering when I became such a helpless women.

Is this what becomes of women when they enter a relationship with someone who is such an energetic take charge kind of guy? This is a big part of why I am so attracted to him, yet I don't want to become a helpless damsel in distress either. Pondering on this as I drive back home, brings to the front of my mind how we as humans are constantly growing, responding and changing to the forces around us. I suppose it's our instincts' at work again, trying to help us survive in an ever changing world.

The night of the Prom finally arrives and after all the to-do, Steph and her date look just like movie stars. The flowers are beautiful and the dress still fits beautifully, as I watch them pose for photos, I can hardly contain myself. They leave the house after reluctantly allowing me to take enough pictures to create a three inch album. Matt teases "You two behave yourselves and you better be home before midnight". "Yeah, right", quips Steph, sticking her tongue out at him as she glides past us.

As I stand in the doorway waving, watching them dash off towards a night they will not soon forget, Steph in her radiant beauty, reminds me of a roaring bonfire. Her youth seems to be burning so brightly it blurs my eyes and warms my heart. As I wipe the tears, I appreciate that another one of her headaches did not emerge to spoil this day.

Just weeks before graduation day, we receive a formal notice from Steph's school. It states that she has been absent too many days of school for them to allow her to graduate with her class. "What"! I know she has missed days or classes due to numerous headache and doctors appointments this semester but we have always sent a note and doctor's excuse. How can this be possible? She has excellent grades; has even been declared exempt from most of her final exams and has continued to be involved in a wide variety of school activities.

Steph says, "I'll talk to my guidance counselor first thing in the morning, I know her the best. I bet she can resolve this." The next morning after talking with her counselor, she is sent to talk with the principle. He tells her even though she had missed quite a few days during the first semester as well, the problem is technically confined to this semester.

He directs us to contact Steph's doctors and request statements explaining the reasons for and the legitimacy of her absences. We contact her primary doctor and the neurologist and they both agree to write statements concerning Stephanie's migraines. In the statement they explain how impossible it can be sometimes to function in a classroom when someone has these episodes. Thinking of how dedicated she has been to keep up her grades throughout high school, I think to myself, "This can not be happening."

After a very stressful week of gathering all the necessary documentation we are informed Steph's case will be presented to the school superintendent for an allowance to be made for her to graduate. The review is scheduled for the next week and poor Steph suffers through several more migraines, though she refuses to miss another class.

Thankfully, she only has a few classes to attend and all Steph's teachers are not only aware of the situation but, prove to be very compassionate and understanding. Each one gave statements affirming that all her given assignments had been completed to date, and most of them allow her to sit in the back of the room with her head down, excusing her from participating in class activities.

Just days before the end of the school year, Steph is asked to come to the principle's office. Nervously she takes a seat, hands clasped tightly in her lap. "Good morning Stephanie, how are you today?" ask the principle. "Fine, Sir, just anxious about my graduation" Steph replies as she forces herself to smile through another migraine. "Well Stephanie, it seems you have a lot of fans in your corner. After a very thorough review, you will be relieved to know the school board has approved you for graduation. Congratulations".

Just before leaving work for lunch, I get a phone call from Steph. "Mom, we did it, it's over. I get to graduate" she says. I can tell she is having trouble holding back her tears of relief by the shakiness in her voice. I feel such joy at the thought of now being able to see her walk across the aisle to receive her diploma. "No Steph, you did it. I'm just so glad this is over" I reply, trying to contain my excitement. My heart feels like it's going to burst.

After all the years of hard work to keep excellent grades, in spite of all her ailments and with such a positive attitude; no one I know deserves this more than my little girl. Isn't this a big part of what it's all about as a parent; seeing your child achieve their goals through adversary.

Graduation week begins with a flurry of excitement madly running through our house. With so many activities making our heads spin, Steph becomes a bit of a scatter brain with things that normally don't fluster her. Simple things like doing her laundry or getting ready for work are suddenly becoming an insurmountable task. I am confused because she has always been so sensible minded and methodically organized.

These commonplace traits seem to have completely abandoned her for some reason. I can only hope that her scatterbrain mindset is simply due to the stress she has been under these last few months. I'll just have to do my best to keep her moving.

Presents arrive, mostly cash and checks along with congratulations for a job well done. I don't concern myself with all the monetary gifts since Steph has always been so fiscally responsible. Her plans are to use the money to help

68

her with the tuition at the community college. She deposits thousands in her checking account and carefully plans her budget and it all seems very reasonable and well thought out to me. She's eighteen now, so of course I believe my job is coming to a close and should let her handle her life as much as possible on her own.

As Steph walks across the stage and receives her diploma my heart swells with pride as one of the great highlights of my life. Seeing her with her friends after the ceremony, all in their cap and gown posing for pictures, hugging everyone and chatting joyously gives me mixed feelings. One side of me is extremely happy and proud for her. The other side realizes with a great sadness that this chapter in her life is coming to a close and my role in her life will only continue to lessen. All day long, I catch myself switching between laughing and crying as we go through our scheduled activities.

We all go though this struggle as our children get older and start to venture out on their own into the world. It can give such a sense of loss and feelings of helplessness now that they seldom turn to us for parental guidance. We all want them to be strong and independent. They have been our unwavering focus for so long, it can be difficult for us to let go of them and loosen the security we have provided for all these years. I'm beginning to see that this is the hardest part of parenting; first finding that fine line, then staying on the appropriate side of that line. Watching; just watching sometimes is all you can do. Where are all the rule books and manuals for that?

Over the next month or so, I find myself a little baffled by some of the things that Steph does and says. Not anything outrageously bizarre, just out of character for her; her room has turned into a mess, dishes and laundry are left all over the place and she's being overly emotional about the most insignificant things. It seems she gets unreasonably upset about simple things, like her pants aren't dry when she wants to wear them or she misses a phone call and they didn't leave a message.

Steph has always been sensitive, but her concern has always been directed towards other's feelings, not herself. I often find myself in a conversation with her and she begins to cry and I haven't a clue why.

I realize some might say that all these scenarios just sound like a typical teenager but keep in mind; Steph never exhibits these types of behaviors. Always the cool calm sensible girl, it just totally puts me at a loss. Mostly it's her emotions that I find unsettling; one minute she's upset to the point of tears about a spot on her shoe and literally the next minute she's giggling and rambling about meeting her friends for a shopping spree.

This is just not my little girl, I can't put my finger on it but something's changing. Sometimes her conversations don't make any sense at all. When she talks, she changes subjects rapidly back and forth so fast, that I have a tough time keeping up with what we're talking about.

I place my hope in trusting that everything will settle down now that the stress of graduation is over, or perhaps a part of me wants to only remember, that for eighteen years Steph has been a model child. Either way, I just can't see beyond what she always has been in the past, and am finding it difficult to focus on what is occurring to her now. I'm not even sure if anything is happening, it's just so confusing.

My dilemma is that Steph has always been the personification of reasoning and determination. Normally she is composed with selfless emotions and has an uncanny aptitude for organization. This is who she is and to accept or recognize anything else is beyond my own sense of what is plausible. It is difficult for me to believe or even allow myself to acknowledge the changes that are appearing, even in such a random pattern.

Trying to persuade Matt that this isn't her normal behavior isn't easy; since he has only really known her for a short while, the situation starts creating tension between us. Every time the topic comes up, the Momma Bear comes out in me and I get defensive about my baby. I know it doesn't help the situation, but this is what we do, isn't it? Anytime someone criticizes our love ones, we focus all our attention on defending them instead of truly getting a solid grasp on what may really be the problem.

I've noticed this phenomenon for years now even if we are the ones who originally brought up the complaint. The moment the other person joins in the criticism, we suddenly forget our own grievances and race to our loved ones defense. Maybe it would be better if the other person really wants to be helpful, if they just kept quiet when we feel the need to vent our frustration. It seems to only make it harder for us to keep our focus on the problem, when we are so busy jumping to the rescue.

On the other hand, maybe those of us with the need to vent, should also be more careful who we vent our frustration too. If we must vent, it seems we need to find very a level headed, non judgmental person who can do just that, just listen. It seems to me, I may be a little to sensitive about Matt's judgments when it comes to my children. I'm suspecting I will need to temper my venting with him so it doesn't become a problem between us.

Phillip, though obviously growing into a sweet, comical, trusting yet somewhat naive young man, continues to struggle in school. His inability to succeed in academics seems to be contributing to his low self-esteem even more so now. His inadequacies revolve around his lack of reading comprehension and that lack causes him to dislike reading even more.

Despite his lack of passing grades in school, he has an innate ability to fix things. He can put anything together after only a glance at the instructions and has the uncanny gift of figuring out how to repair anything broken in the household. He just looks at the task and can quickly access the needed repair. Since moving into our home he has easily installed new toilets, faucets, even a thermo coupler for the heater. Gladly, I make a big deal out of his talents, it's a big help to me and I love that it also seems to boost his self esteem.

Steph's headaches are becoming more and more frequent. She is sleeping so much lately. I know when a migraine comes upon her it's the only thing that helps, but lately it seems to me all she does is sleep. When I ask her about it, she tells me sleeping is all that helps and the headaches make her tired all the time. I'm so frustrated with this change in her but I can't help worrying about her.

As weeks pass, I notice one week she's sleeping a lot and then the next week she's running all over the place with an enormous amount of energy. Watching her from week to week reminds me of a child's wind up toy. One of those types that run all over the floor spastically then abruptly comes to a sudden stop. Unable to move until someone comes along and winds it up again, providing an unseen power for it to run around in circles for a little while longer. It's exhausting just watching her, as well as confusing.

As happens with many parents when they don't live with their children, Mike has become less and less involved in both Phillip and Stephanie's lives. Oh, I know he loves and thinks of them, but his participation in their day to day life has dwindled considerably in the last few years. Since they became teenagers and started driving, they have spent less time with him, which naturally would diminish any relationship. It takes a lot of time and effort spent nosing into the other's affairs to continue any close connection.

Looking back, I realize I should have encouraged them both to make more of an effort to stay connected. Now, I even feel so distant from Mike myself, that it feels awkward for me to even bring these latest issues to his attention. Mike and I rarely speak to each other and since our children are in their teens, I've not felt a need to stay in the forefront of their relationship. When it comes to explaining what's going on, I don't know where to start. A big part of me, still hopes this problem is just my imagination.

Life at home is not getting any easier with Matt continually questioning me about Steph's behavior. I have difficulty describing to him the differences in how she is acting now and how she normally is. All he sees is this bizarre behavior; he really doesn't understand that it is all new bizarre behavior. Most of these actions are difficult for me to explain, much less understand.

Phillip withdraws more and more from Steph. In fact he seems withdrawn from the entire household and more moody too. He is rarely home, whether at work or out with his friends, I seldom know which. His school work continues to suffer and it's all I can do now, to get him to take the trash out. Too many things are changing, too many things for me to focus on.

All I can think about is, this is not who Steph is. She alternates between irrational moods, to random chattering, to crying at the drop of a hat, and I can't decipher a logical pattern to any of it. My home is turning into a congressional squabble fest and all I want to do is protect my little girl from further analysis.

Then, just when I start to think something is seriously wrong, Steph turns back into her old self, calm cool and collected just taking care of business. I see her clear headedness and the return of her radiant smile as an opportunity. I ask, "What going on with you, honey? You haven't been yourself lately." Steph replies, "What do you mean Mom? I'm fine, well, except for the headaches". As I try to describe to her some of the scenarios that have given me such concern lately, her only response is, "What are you talking about?" Her radiant smile quickly melts away.

With a puzzled look on her face, she just looks at me like I've lost my mind. Huh, maybe I have, she seems fine now. Maybe I'm just imagining all this craziness, in my need to have something to worry about. This craziness goes on for another week or so; back and forth we go between the old reality I've known for eighteen years and something else that makes no sense to me at all.

Fall brings the start of school and Steph registers for community college, signing up for a full load of classes. I find myself cautiously relieved, thinking maybe things will get back to some sort of normalcy. We continue to tiptoe around the difficulties we experienced this past summer and hope for the best. Sometimes though, all our hopes can be for naught.

I spend half my time trying to protect Steph from Matt's prying observations and the other half being frustrated with some of the new behaviors she's exhibiting. Most of the time, I can talk to Matt about anything but not this is topic. We are just not able to see eye to eye when it comes to Stephanie. I find myself getting more and more defensive. "Matt", I plead, "You just don't understand. This is not how she normally acts." "Please just let it go, she's seeing a therapist."

One example of the change I see in Steph, involves money. As I have said, Steph has always been very responsible with money. Responsible to the point, that for several years I let her carry my own debit card so she can help me do the grocery shopping. I never had a second thought about what my little coupon clipper spent. In the two years that she's had her own check book, she has not once bounced a check or had a problem paying any of her bills.

Checking the mail today, I found several envelopes from credit card companies addressed to Steph. I can tell the difference in a credit card statement and an offer, these are definitely statements. She has been shopping a lot lately but I haven't thought too much about it until now, so when she comes home, I privately ask her about them. As she shrugs my concern off, she says "Don't worry Mom, I'm just trying to build my credit".

A few weeks later a few more come in the mail, and then by the end of the next month, six different statements have arrived. As I press her for a better explanation, Steph finally spills the beans, "I applied for a bunch of credit cards when I was shopping and I was approved for all of them." Continuing my inquisition, I discover that she has now maxed all of them out.

As I quietly sit there in shock and disbelief, the reality of the situation seems to suddenly be sinking in with Steph. With a surprisingly confused look on her face, she spills more of the beans. "I would pay them off with some of my graduation money but I spent all of it. I don't even remember what I bought." As the quiet lengthens between us, my heart leaps to my throat. "What! What did you say? Could you repeat that?" I exclaim. I can't help thinking to myself, "Where did this come from? Who is this person and where is my daughter?"

Apparently, Steph is holding even more beans. "Mom, she meekly asks, "can you help me with my checkbook; I haven't been able to balance it this past months." Seeing a look of anxiety in her face, cautiously I take the register from her. This is the first time she's asked me to help her with it, since I showed her how to reconcile it with her first statement. After that first lesson, she only showed it to me a few times to confirm that she was doing it correctly. That was over two years ago.

As I take a look, I'm puzzled by the last two or three pages of entries. Where before, all entries were written in her neat script and deducted or added correctly, the last few pages are a mess of totally incomprehensible scribbles. There are no dates in some places, no amounts in others, and the handwriting doesn't even appear to be hers. Her register looks as if an eight years old child has taken it over.

Looking into Steph's eyes, I see a scared little girl. Normally, in a situation such as this, I would at least ask a few questions. But seeing her in this unusually fragile state, I haven't the heart to put her through any interrogation. Three hours later, I am still not able to reconcile her bank account. At work, I have never been unable to reconcile an account.

In an attempt to make light of the situation I suggest, "Well, you've got me stumped honey, I guess I'm not as smart as I think I am. Let's just wait a week and let everything clear the bank. I'll give you a little cash to use and then we can just start a new register next week. Don't use you debit card or write another check, okay?" With a forced half smile, she simply replies "Okay, thanks Mom".

Two days later, I find her at my desk with what looks to be a stack of bills, looking for stamps. "Are you mailing bills?" I ask. "I thought we agreed to let your account settle." Steph looks over at me with an annoyed look on her face and says, "I know what I'm doing, Mom."

Trying to have a conversation with Steph about her checking account becomes a nightmare. She is irrational and indignant, telling me she can handle it and I should butt out of her business. She has a big plan to solve her debt. Even though her debt is only a few hundred dollars on each card, I know using credit cards so freely can easily snow ball into enormous amounts.

But her plan makes no sense; in fact, not much of what she says is making any sense. She's just rambling on and on about a wide range of different topics. We are getting no where and then suddenly, she declares she's going to bed; where she stays for two full days.

I spend the next two days, getting little sleep and trying to remember the sequence of events of the last few months. The ups and downs have kept me so confused, so off balance that I can't make sense of any of it. I realize it's not been a pretty picture and our house has become a semi-war zone, with me trying to portray the part of Switzerland. I know in the core of my being, something is wrong. I only wish I knew what that 'something' was. Nevertheless, I foolishly I still want to cling to the hope that this too shall pass.

Saturday morning, after my coffee, I go up to Steph's room to see if she has finally decided to get out of bed so we can talk. She has pulled almost all her clothes out of her closet and tossed them in crumpled stacks. Everything has been taken down from her walls and strewn outside her room.

Her bed is stripped and only by close scrutiny do I find her bundled up in the corner behind her bed on the floor in her favorite comforter. Her eyes have a wild intense scared look about them. Twitching uncontrollably, she's staring off into space and mumbling. I suddenly realize I don't know who is frightened more, me or my little girl.

As I gingerly move towards her, she doesn't even look up at me. Not sure what's really happening or what to do; I just sit down beside her. Trying my best to stay calm, I slowly wrap my arms around her and pull her to my chest. Steph's trembling body slightly relaxes as I kiss her forehead and stroke her hair. For a brief moment I am confused by the wetness of her forehead, until I become conscious of my own tears.

As I take a few deep breaths, both Steph and I regain some measure of control. I continue to comb her hair with my fingers and whisper to her, "Its okay honey, everything will be fine, just fine." In my mind I'm thinking – "Fine, I don't even know what's happening, how can anything be fine?" Somewhere, something deep inside me a flame begins to burn – ever so slowly -the spirit of motherhood soothes my fears. I don't know how to fix this, but I do know one thing, somehow – someway – we'll try to fix this together.

Not since Steph was small child, have I felt the need to be so protective, so fiercely determined to destroy this unknown intruder. But, first things, first, to begin with I must figure out what the problem even is. After a while, her grip loosens on the blanket so I slowly pull Steph to her feet and onto her bed. Gently covering her, I kiss her temples and whisper, "You rest now honey, I'll be right down stairs." "I'll check back on you in a little bit."

Precariously, I go downstairs in search of Matt. As I describe what I just found upstairs to Matt, a rare stillness comes over him. After months of watching my daughter disintegrate into God knows what, my take-charge kind of guy sits me down and calmly tells me, I must get Steph the help she needs. "She's been seeing a Psychologist for months. Wouldn't she know what's wrong?" I ask.

Matt leans into me, puts his hand over mine and says, "No, not necessarily, listen to me, if all you're telling me about Steph's past behavior is true, then something drastic could be happening to her mind. Only a Psychiatrist will be able to diagnose and treat her. You have to get her to a Psychiatrist."

The very word, Psychiatrist, is a frightening word, at least to me. I've never known anyone who has been to see one, never known anyone who needed one. At least I don't think I have. Just having Steph see a Psychologist has been a stretch for me, but a Psychiatrist? Aren't they for crazy people? What does this mean? That I must accept that Steph is crazy?

Of course I don't want to hear it, but Matt has chosen this particular time to be the epitome of reasoning and objectivity. As I listen to his words, try to listen to my heart, I close my eyes, I can still vividly see my precious child clutching her blanket. As I dance around this idea, he gently but firmly closes the deal and sets us of on a course that I never could have imagined.

I believe God has sent this man to me just in time, for this very purpose. I don't think I can face this reality alone.

Though just hearing this suggestion knocks the wind out of me, somewhere deep inside me I know this statement rings as true as knowing the sun will shine again tomorrow.

After pulling myself together, I go back upstairs to tell Steph about our decision. I present it to her gently but firmly, without any latitude for other options. I tell her, I know in my heart something is terribly wrong and we must find out what that something is. She surprises me by saying; she also knows something is wrong; she just feels like she's losing her mind. It seems that Steph gains strength just from the admission, gains courage from the hope that help could be, just around the corner.

First thing Monday morning I make an appointment for Steph with a prominent Dallas Psychiatric Center. Having to wait two more days until her appointment is tearing me apart. I can't stop thinking about all the various scenarios that are playing havoc with my mind making feel as if it's going to explode. My heart is in my throat and I can't seem to take a full breath of air. My hands shake so much I drop almost everything I pick up. Though she does seem more in control of her self, I'm afraid to let her out of my sight; controlling my own emotions is becoming harder by the minute.

I can't stop thinking about my baby. How and why would this even be happening? Will our lives ever return to some recognizable form of our past? Will this doctor be able to help us? What if he has no idea what's wrong or worse, what if this can't be fixed? I don't know very much about mental illnesses in general. But I think these types of problems must be more complicated to treat than having a clear cut diagnosable disease.

After looking on several internet sites that describe mental illnesses, I have learned a little more about these types of issues. I have discovered a big part of the diagnosis will depend on if Steph is even able to tell him what's wrong. How she feels and what she thinks, apparently will give important clues to the problem.

So, my child will sit in a room with a professional, whom I hope is as good as all the degrees on the wall indicate and try to spill her guts. Will she be open and honest? Can she even attempt to explain what's going on? How can she possibly give any insight into this dilemma? Steph's more confused than I am at this point, not to mention scared out of her mind.

It's confusing enough just trying to figure out where to go, when you finally acknowledge that something's wrong. Now I must not only accept the probability that my daughter is suffering from some type of mental problem but, I must and I repeat must come to an understanding about conditions that use more complicated words than are in my current vocabulary. Not to mention that it's difficult to get a concrete diagnosis, like "my child has a broken leg". It doesn't take a brain surgeon to know the thing's broken when the bone is sticking out or bent like a boomerang.

Meanwhile, your waiting for what you hope is a quick fix of some kind, a rare vitamin deficiency or for someone to say oh, you've misunderstood, she just needs more attention. That I could do, but this, no, this I'm sure will require much more than just my attention.

CHAPTER 6 Fall 1999

While waiting for the diagnosis, I seem to be constantly alternating between crying and frantically pacing around. Matt has again willingly become, my sole support in this crisis. He tries his best to calm me and soothe my tears by telling me that she will be in the best possible hands for these types of issues. "Let's just wait and see what's wrong, and then we'll take it from there." He says. I'm having a difficult time buying into any of his comforting words, my baby is falling apart and the belief that anything will ever be the same again is a hard sell.

Before today I've never heard much about the term, Bipolar, much less the rest of her diagnosis. After being more honest and frank than ever in her life, Steph is told after a three hour consult that what she has, is known as Bipolar 1, ultra-rapid cycling with psychotic episodes. I am at loss as to what any of this means and am completely taken aback and terrified by the word psychotic.

The Psychiatrist tells her that even though her condition is quite serious, her honesty and openness in the consult will give her a head start from most people with this type of disorder. He continues to tell her normally, those with any form of Bipolar disorder hide from the truths and bury themselves in denial or are too ill to even recognize that there is a problem, therefore go undiagnosed for many years before they even seek the help they need. Those with Bipolar 1 present an even greater challenge.

Steph takes a deep breath and the quietly admits to me that she also told the doctor that in the past she has practiced Bulimia to control her weight. Looking back on the last few years, I am stunned that I never saw or considered this as the source to her stomach problems and weight loss. I'm confused as to how I, a mother who thought she was so in tune with her child, could have missed all the clues. The old saying appears to be a sound one; you don't see the Forrest for the Trees.

I'm a bit stunned by Steph's calmness as she explains to me everything the doctor has told her about her illness. To me, she seems very serine and at peace with it all, like a weight has been lifted off her shoulders and placed on her doctors. Then Steph stands up and says she's drained and would just like to go to bed and get some rest. I hug her goodnight and reassure her that we will get through this together.

As I watch her climb the stairs, I become angry, heartbroken, perplexed, you name it; I'm feeling it and can't seem to get a handle on any of my emotions. Thankfully Matt takes me aside; he sees that I need to hear tough words to get my attention focused back on Steph.

Hearing that I must put myself on the back burner if I am to be any help to my daughter, I take a deep breath and do as my mother has said for years, "just keep putting one foot in front of the other."

Matt and I decide the first thing we need to do, is get a full understanding of Steph's condition and as usual I turn to the internet in search of more descriptive information. I am even more disturbed, as I review the numerous statistics on the stability rate, psychotic episodes and suicide rate of those with this disorder. Can it really be as devastating as this?

I scan the articles supplied by various medical websites and the information I uncover bombards me with feelings of hopelessness and despair. How can any parent come to terms with the heart wrenching discovery that their child has this terrible disorder? What I learn about the incurable disorder my daughter has just been diagnosed with and must somehow learn to live with for the remainder of her life, is devastating to me.

I quickly discover that Bipolar disorder is a mental illness that affects a person's thoughts, feelings, perceptions and behavior ... even how a person can feel physically. Articles tell me it's believed to possibly be caused by electrical and chemical elements in the brain not functioning properly. However, years of research will be needed to fully understand how this disorder really works.

As I get to the specifics of Steph's diagnosis, Bipolar 1 I recognize the resemblance. It's defined as a person who has had both full blown depression and full blown mania episodes portraying moods that shift from severe highs to severe lows and back again in varying degrees and frequency. Well, that seems to fit Steph to a tee. As I read on, I scan the symptoms that reveal depression and mania to varying degrees.

Depression can be identified by:

- Refusing to get out of bed for days on end

- Sleeping much more than usual

- Being tired all the time but unable to sleep

- Having bouts of uncontrollable crying

- Becoming entirely uninterested in things you once enjoyed

- Paying no attention to daily responsibilities

83

- Feeling hopeless, helpless or worthless for a sustained period of time

- Becoming unable to make simple decisions

- Wanting to die

Mania can include:

- Feeling like you can do anything, even something unsafe or illegal

- Needing very little sleep, yet never feeling tired

- Dressing flamboyantly, spending money extravagantly, living recklessly

- Having increased sexual desires, perhaps even indulging in risky sexual behaviors

- Experiencing hallucinations or delusions

- Feeling filled with over abundance of energy

I find this website as overwhelming as it is helpful. Reading on it seems that some people think that they are just "over their depression" when they become manic, and don't realize this exaggerated state is just another part of their illness. When I get to the part that explains when these manic episodes, left unchecked can run completely out of control I recognize Steph in the symptoms.

It goes on to explain that Bipolar 1 Disorder is more than just wide ranging mood swings. Some of the more complex features of this disorder are described to include: Rapid cycling is when episodes occur four times or more per year. And Ultra-rapid cycling is described as episodes occurring monthly or even more frequently.

My hands begin to shake as I read the last two descriptions of Steph's diagnosis. Bipolar 1 can also have very frightening characteristics of psychosis or a loss of contact with reality. Yes, it seems to me that she has defiantly lost contact with reality a few times. Then reading on I get a huge pit in my stomach as I read the characteristics that psychosis can include:

- Hallucinations - hearing or seeing things that are not there

- Delusions - persistent beliefs in things that are not true

- Paranoia - believing that a person or group is actively working to harm you, without any basis in fact.

It seems that many suffering with this disorder go untreated for years, to only find them selves' homeless, alienated from family, self medicating through alcohol and /or drugs or end up in mental institutions. And they warn that these are the ones who are able to survive thus far. Reading on I see what they mean.

My heart stops as begin to comprehend one of the most dangerous aspects of Bipolar 1. The danger's of suicide. Statistics show that the suicide rate among those with Bipolar disorder are as high as twenty percent, which means a staggering number of them make unsuccessful and/or repeated attempts on their own lives, and even more of them consider suicide without acting on the urge.

All this information scares me out of my mind. Just the thought that Stephanie has possibly had any of these horrifying thoughts (delusions or suicide especially) breaks my heart. How do I protect her from this? How can anyone ever be protected from such an illness?

Seeing that mental illnesses typically run in families, I make a mental note to check to see if anyone can remember anyone on both sides of Steph's family tree has had any form of mental illness. Mentally, I run through my siblings, cousins, aunts, uncles looking for some sign or trace of any mental illness. I can't remember anyone in my family who really even seems to get depressed.

Now at least I have a better grasp on what's been happening to Steph, though I still have no idea if she has been experiencing all the symptoms. Just looking back over all those strange scenarios and after reading medical articles in mass quantity, it all makes so much more sense to me now. Well, maybe not total sense, but at least it explains some of her bizarre behavior lately. As I think to myself, at least I know now that I'm not crazy, my heart sinks to a new low. As I realize what just ran through my head, I burst into tears. My daughter is crazy.

After drying my eyes and blowing my nose, I take a deep breath and continue on. I also discover that a high percentage of people with Bipolar I are often highly intelligent, extraordinarily gifted, and glowingly talented - people whose brilliance can make the world a better place, while they themselves struggle every day to cope, to function, and even just stay alive.

I am amazed to discover that some of our most famous painters, composers, authors, entrepreneurs and inventors are believed to have suffered from this illness. So is this supposed to be some sort of consolation prize or the price one pays for being extraordinary?

Spending all these hours at the computer has filled my head with way to much information to coherently digest it all properly. I've never been one to get down about things,

Mama always stressed that one should always try to look on the bright side but this has certainly done the job.

But once again, Matt redirects my attention to the problem at hand. He tells me, "You can't let this get you down, you're daughter needs you strong now, more than ever." He reminds me, "just think about it, if we are having a difficult time digesting this, just try and imagine how Steph would be feeling after learning what has been dealt to her."

Over the next few days I try and get a better grasp on what the doctor told Steph. She admits to being scared of what this means for her but, says with a slight confidence that she believes with her doctors' help, she will learn how to deal with it. I get the feeling that just the thought of having a professional who understands this illness has helped her regain some of her old composure, for the moment at least. Like he has thrown her a life jacket and she is clinging to it as if her life depends on it, maybe it does.

Apparently the doctor thought she should be hospitalized at first. Then after discussing her condition more with her, he agreed to let her come home with us and a promise from her to return in four days. During the second appointment he discusses a wide variety of new medicines out now that are showing promising results and he gives her three prescriptions. The main problem with this he says will be that it may take a while to find the right mix, so to speak, for her. You see, everyone has a different chemical make up and what works for one person may not for another.

Now I must make a few phone calls, the first one to her father who has no idea any of this has been going on. Not knowing what to tell him these past months, I have kept silent, now I'm not sure where to start. After listening to me babble, sobbing through most of it, He takes the news in his usual matter of fact way. Considering the shock of this news about our daughter, I find myself somehow calmed by his detached stance. He agrees to check on his family history for any sign of mental illnesses. We end our conversation with his promise to continue to keep her on his insurance plan as long as Texas State law allows.

My next call is to Mama, who I also have not mentioned any of the bizarre behavior Steph's been portraying for the last few months. She quietly listens to me ramble on about what's been happening, though I'm not at all sure I'm making any sense. The more I talk, the more I find that I wish I had confided in her from the beginning. I just never wanted to worry her when I didn't even understand myself what was going on.

As usual Mama reminds me "As bad as this seems, it could be worse. Steph could have cancer or any number of terminal illnesses." "We could even be living back in a time when this particular was not understood as well as it is now." As in many other times in my life Mama calms me, supports me and helps me regain a clear perspective on the crisis at hand. As I hang up she reminds me "Just keep putting on foot in front of the other, just keep moving. And above all things just cling to thought that it could be worse."

Why is it, when we feel the most like we're all alone in this world, if we just stand still for a moment we can always find people standing strong with us, sometimes for us? Why is it we tend to think we must handle a crisis all by ourselves when our loved ones are so readily available to us for support? I am discovering that I don't have to be super mom; I don't have to have all the answers, just keep holding on to the glimmer of hope that maybe in time as Mama always says, "This too shall pass."

Over the course of my life, I have known and have heard stories of other parents in the unfathomable position of having one of their children suffering from severe illnesses. Almost all parents have witnessed the heartache seen so readily on the faces of those in such tragic situations, so it's not difficult to imagine my anguish and the desperation I feel to help my child. We have all put ourselves in those helpless parents place mentally for a moment, and felt a taste of their pain as we let our imagination run wild. I am quickly discovering though that the reality is much worse than our imagination can allow.

All during this crisis, Matt and I have tried our best to continue to perform all the normal functions grownups are required to do on a daily basis. The stresses of day to day life for any parent with two teens can be complex enough. Then add to it our jobs that are each riddled with their own mix of pressure and our fairly new relationship, you can easily imagine the overwhelming strain that comes with all we are now trying to handle.

I often have a difficult time concentrating on any given task at work for more than a few minutes at a time. Yet part of me, greatly appreciates the temporary escape, when I'm able to set aside the fear of what is happening at home and focus on tangible problems that I can actually solve. It reminds me of another one of Mama's phrases, "Sometimes just trying to help resolve someone else's problems can help take your mind off your own problems." Thankfully my accounting position at work provides plenty of other problems to solve.

When Steph returns to her psychiatrist the next week, he discusses with her how she is doing with her new prescriptions. More specifically, how she feels about the anti-depressant he had given her to hopefully help her regain control over her depression. He warns again that she will most likely have to try out several medications for depression until they find one that works best for her.

Also he had prescribed an anti-seizure medication called Depakote. It has been discovered recently that anticonvulsant medications help patients with Bipolar 1 who "rapid cycle" with their mood swinging more than four times a year. This particular medication, he said, has shown promising results recently and he wants to see how she responds to it. An added benefit to this drug is the hope of reducing migraines.

In addition to those two medications he had also prescribed an anti-psychotic drug with the hope of diminishing that dreadful feature of her disorder. Again He stresses that more than likely she will need to try out several of these types' of medications until one is found that works best for her. So the trial and error period has begun and all we can do is watch and wait to see how each of these drugs affects her.

The first few weeks are full of anxiety for all of us as we keep an eye on Steph and how she is responding to the prescribed treatment. For the most part she seems to be a little more stable, a little calmer and less sporadic. Though she still is not the same young lady who can take on the world, I am slightly comforted that she is no longer dealing with it alone, trapped inside her own turmoil.

I find it relieving; just to have an answer for her bizarre behavior and that she now has a professional working with her that understand what's happening. I'm spending all my free time reading everything I can get my hands on, both from the internet and the library, which gives insight to this disorder that, has taken over our household. I find most of the information to be very helpful in explaining the wide ranges of behaviors and what danger signs to look out for. I am beginning to realize that this will be a lifelong commitment for both of us.

It seems I must be making everyone in the house a little crazy with my fixation about Steph's condition, including Steph. As I try to review with Steph some of the latest information she comments to me, "Mom, I don't want my entire life to be about being Bipolar. I know you mean well but sometimes you need to just give it a rest." As I listen to her, really listen, I get the feeling that though she appreciates my efforts, I am overwhelming her with information every day; I just can't seem to stop myself.

I want so badly to be able to fix this for her, and my inability to do that, is more frustrating than anything I have ever experienced in my life. I talk about it all the time, obsess about it would be a better word. It is emotionally and mentally exhausting but I feel I must persist; this issue and how to cope with it, is the sole purpose for me getting up every day.

Frustration overwhelms me as my search in both family histories for the root cause of this illness comes up blank. No one in either Steph's father's family or mine has ever known anyone with any form of a mental illness other than some mild depression on her Dad's side. My mind is torn in a bitter battle trying to find not only an answer for why but also how this could have happened. On a deeper level, I think I need some place to put the blame. I wonder has Steph's mental illness been triggered somehow by her head injury last year. I can't seem to find a definitive answer to these questions.

A twisted part of me even wants to place the blame on myself for allowing this to happen to my baby. Matt insists, "It's not helping you or Steph, obsessing about why or how. You have to find a way to put all these questions to rest so you can stay focused on the problem." In my mind, I know he's right; my obsession with finding the cause is only sucking energy away from me, energy that is desperately needed elsewhere.

Thinking this through, I realize that the way I'm dealing with this situation is similar to dealing with a death or fatal illness and the grieving process you go through. Though I think I have finally passed through the denial stage, I guess I must be stuck in the anger stage. So, deciding not to let it get in my way of helping Steph in this crisis, I choose to put this anger in a box, high up on a shelf; very, very high up on a shelf.

Turning my energy to more productive things, I search the internet for helpful information on how to deal with this illness. Coming across a website specifically for people with Bipolar and/or Manic Depression, I notice a

91

support group page. Hum, this might be helpful. As I peruse the information; I notice it has support group meetings for the entire family. Waiting for the page to print, I plot the next step in approaching Steph.

After work the next day, while sitting on the porch with Matt, Steph arrives home. Her mood seems good so as she sits down with us, I make my move. "Hey, I found this Bipolar support group that meets once a month." Seeing an interested look on her face I quickly continue, "They work towards helping the patient and their families understand and deal with your type of illness. Do you want to go check it out?"

Taken a bit by surprise, Steph asked, "Where and when is it, but I don't want to go by myself. What do they do at these meetings?" Feeling relieved just hearing her interest in this; I excitedly push forward, "Next Saturday at three o'clock somewhere near Baylor Hospital, but I'm not really sure what they do other than having a speaker and open discussions."

Matt surprises us both by saying, "Maybe we should all go. It's worth giving it a try, don't you guys think?" As Steph and I look at each other, then over to Matt, he says, "Well? Come on, let's do it, it couldn't hurt." With a lump in my throat, tears in Steph's eyes, all we can do, is nod. Matt, being the take charge kind of guy that he is, just smiles as his pronouncement is agreed upon.

Matt is turning out to be much more supportive than I ever could have imagined. I often find myself thinking to myself that I would not have wanted to live through this crisis without him. Before we knew what was going on with Steph, she and her behavior had become such a thorny issue between us. It seems that now knowing what is wrong with her, Matt has pushed aside all those unwanted thorns and joined forces with us.

We arrive at our first meeting full of expectations, with the hope that these meetings will give each of us some sense of direction in the individual roles we are to play. Hope that these meetings will show us, that just maybe this monster we are struggling with, can be tamed into manageable submission.

As we locate the proper meeting room, I glance over at Steph, wondering how she is feeling. My heart pinches as I recall the days not so very long ago, when she would be the one in the forefront of our little group. Striding confidently into the room, with that brilliant smile of hers catching everyone's attention. But not today, today she hangs back, self-conscious apprehension and anxiety written all over her face.

As the meeting is called to order, out of the corner of my eye, I notice Steph scooted down low in her seat, looking around curiously at the other attendees. I get the feeling she is comparing herself to them, or looking for some sign that tells her, these are just normal people, that she is going to be normal again. But then again, maybe it just me; maybe I'm the one looking to see some confirmation that people with Bipolar can pull through this, that my baby can return to a normal life.

I've spent so much time just learning what Bipolar is, the symptoms, the things to watch for, the statistics. Yet, I've spent little time looking for the tools people use to live with it day to day. I anxiously await the guest speaker, for him to shed some light on what it is they do to help them cope and survive.

The opening discussion is given by a tall heavy-set man in his late fifties. He tells the fifty or so people in the auditorium his life story and how he has been affected by his mental illness. He has Bipolar or, as he clarifies with us, what used to be referred to simply as Maniac-Depression. With greater psychiatric understanding, he tells us, these illnesses

93

are now better defined, allowing for symptoms to be categorized more specifically.

As he describes his life as full of grandiose bizarre adventures, I'm waiting to hear how he copes and stays stable. Thirty minutes into his story and I'm still waiting. No helpful hints, just a long rendition of his delusional crazy life, told almost pompously, like he felt a certain pride in his life.

Maybe it's just me, but I can't help but think, I wouldn't be proud of putting my family in such financially precarious danger. Nor do I think I would be proud that I could convince people into investing huge amounts of money into an imagined company.

Even though he admits his mind was out of balance at the time, I listen closely for some regret, some sign of self-loathing. Nope, instead he turns the speech towards the use of medication. My ears perk up, at last, some direction. Nope, he tells the crowd he continually struggles with taking his medication because he feels it hinders his creativity.

In shock I think to myself, "Oh, my God, does he want the mania to reign free?" Could that really be helpful, am I missing something here? As my eyes and ears glaze over, my mind drifts in the anticipation of hope from the promised support group share time that is coming up next.

Another half hour later, as we move to our assigned group area for share time, a quick glimpse at Steph reveals a wide eyed apprehension. Well, at least we're still on the same wave length. I wonder what Matt's thinking about all this, he looks as if he desperately wants to go have a cigarette. But then again with his Hyper Type "A" nature, he always looks like he wants a cigarette, sort of like a caged lion seeking to escape back into the wild.

Sitting in a circle listening to each participant, it sort of feels like I'm at an AA meeting, you know, "Hi, I'm Bob and I'm a Bipolar". Each one telling of the wild and crazy life they proudly lead, seemingly each trying to out do the last person. I'm getting the impression that each of them wears their illness like a badge of honor, almost bragging about the troubles they create for their families.

As the group session takes a short break, Steph, Matt and I huddle in the hall to compare thoughts. The look on Matt's face tells me he's had enough, just as I have. I'm not so sure this has been all that helpful. Maybe some people need to just have someone to hear them vent, but I was hoping for more practical direction. But we are here for Steph's benefit after all, so I ask "What do you think, Steph? Is this helping you?"

As she shrugs her shoulders, then looks around, and whispers to me, "I'm ready to go, if ya'll are. I don't need to hear any more of their stories; I thought this would give me some ideas as to what else I should be doing." Her voice betrays the same disappointment that I feel.

On the drive home we decide not to return for their next meeting. Maybe, it's just the new emersion into this nightmare that distorts our view. While I'm sure these types of meetings help many people with this disorder, we all agree it is not for us. At least not for now, what we are looking for is more practical advice. As with all problems, each of us must find our own path and use what works for us.

Since the beginning of Steph's diagnosis, the one fundamental principle we all agree on is in the belief that having a mental illness could be, should be in fact viewed and dealt with as any other major illness. If Steph had been diagnosed as a diabetic she would have to find a way to live in this world with it and the same is true for being Bipolar.

Steph's own mindset about her illness is to get stable, remain stable and get on with her life. She is determined to not let this take over her existence as the people in her group seem to. That alone gives me an abundance of hope, that attitude is so much like My Stephanie.

As the months pass we all develop and settle into our own individual support roles. Matt is as the always understanding and reasonable support for me, available to allow me to collapse on him at a moments notice. He seems to be consciously or unconsciously not involving himself in Steph's day to day care. Instead he focuses his energy on helping to keep me sane and focused.

Phillip, who I don't believe, fully understands what's happening to his sister, is increasingly distant and busy with his own agenda. Talking to him about Steph only seems to aggravate him. He scoots in and out of the house so inconspicuously, it's almost like he wants to hide from view. It's like he needs time to sort this all out in his mind.

As for myself, I'm not really sure how to describe what I have become. Most of the time, I find myself trying to be the brave steady rock that I feel I have to be for Steph. I fully admit though, that I allow myself to be a complete basket case when she's not around. Thankfully, Matt seems to be strong enough to hold me up, pull me back together and encourage me on my way.

I am fascinated by the fact that all of us can usually find the strength, fortitude and support to deal with life's trials when it is necessary. I do believe, in each of us is a powerful force that we have available to tap into, if we reach down deep, in our time of need. I often find myself wondering, if we could just foster that ability on a more consistent basis, what more astounding things we could accomplish as human beings.

Steph continues to see her doctor every two weeks to discuss how the meds are working. I'm glad he's keeping such a close eye on her mental state and seems to know when to make adjustments as needed. Her doctor switches her anti-depressant several times, trying to get her depression under control. He has left her on the depakote to stabilize her mood and the same anti-psychotic, not wanting to switch too many medications at one time. I think that makes good sense.

However, we are all still very anxious to see if these medications can help her regain some resemblance of her old self.

My schedule from day to day now consist of waking up, getting ready for work, going upstairs to attempt to wake up Steph, giving her the morning meds, waking her up again before I leave for work. Then once I get to work I call Steph to see if she woke up, then I worry most of the day as to whether she actually did wake up.

After work I often come home to find her, asleep in bed with her meds and juice still setting on her nightstand. On the days that I don't find her home, I feel brief excitement that she made it up in time for work. But it's not long before I start stressing again. Will she make it home in time to take her nightly meds so I can tuck her in for the night? Day after day it's the same scenario. Day after day we must start the same cycle over and over again.

I know this all sounds like a little mommy overkill, but I'm consumed with the idea of getting her stable, so she can regain some sense of a normal life. I have become, at least in my own eyes, her lifeline to reality and am determined to do all that I can to help her put the pieces back together. I have turned into such a control freak, anxiously pretending to have some power over this monster that has taken control of my daughter and our home.

Sure there are some days where she seems a little more like her old self, but that likeness is so very little. All in all, I have to say that she has really turned into a completely different person. I am so frustrated and bewildered with who she has become, so much so, that sometimes my reactions to her are harsh and unsympathetic. It is often difficult for me to separate the anger that I feel towards this illness from how I feel about my daughter.

I have to remind her over and over about appointments and responsibilities that the old Steph would have handled with ease. No longer is she the organized, self-disciplined and determined young lady I have counted on for years. She has lost that caring, compassionate, affectionate and lighthearted nature that had consoled me during my father's illness and death. It is all I can do, to get even a half-hug out of her. Many of the core traits that defined who she was seem to have dissolved, so much so that I hardly recognize her anymore. For so long I've counted on her being such a success in her life, now I am fearful for every aspect of her life.

For the most part, I don't think people appreciate having medical insurance until they are faced with a serious medical issue themselves. As anyone would in this circumstance, I continually worry about Steph's insurance which is currently provided by her father. Mike works for the county and has a fairly good plan, but my concern is with how often the county changes plans. Every year as all companies do, his plan is reviewed by the human resources department and some changes are made.

In my own position at work I deal with this process and am very familiar with what happens when a company changes insurance plans. Often times the company changes not just plans within insurance companies but will switch insurance companies all together. This can be a huge concern when you have a condition that requires regular monitoring by your doctor. While many doctors take many insurance plans, that isn't always the case. Then you are forced to select another doctor, spend a few months getting comfortable with him all the while, hoping he knows what he's doing.

My other concern is the requirement the county has concerning the coverage of adult children. They require them to be enrolled full time in college to be eligible for coverage on a parents plan. Steph enrolled in college the beginning of the semester but has only sporadically been able to attend classes and has since dropped out of most of them. Will this mean that her coverage could be cancelled?

Nor is she able to work a consistent schedule at a job, and has switched employment twice already in an attempt to find something with enough flexibility to accommodate her illness. It's only a matter of time until someone fires her due to excessive absences. Which bring to my mind another concern; will my baby ever be able to finish school, hold down a full time job or have any form of a normal life?

All these worries constantly race through my head; my job, Steph's illness, her job, her school, her insurance, Phillips continued withdrawal, my new relationship with Matt, it's a wonder I don't need medication. I bounce back and forth between trying to have some form of acceptance, to a frustrated sense of denial that this nightmare is happening to our family.

I feel like my ability to focus on any one task has been greatly diminished. My entire focus is on Steph and her stability, her very survival. I admit it; in my concern for my oldest child I am letting other things go unnoticed. My capacity to handle all things, be all things, to all who need me is falling by the wayside. It's devastating to look myself in the mirror, no longer able see the woman who can handle anything and everything. The reality is that I am going to need all of the help I can get to face this monster that has invaded our lives.

I am obsessed with making sure Steph takes her medicine every day. I bought two of those pill boxes at the pharmacy the other day, labeled Monday through Sunday to put her meds in for the week. We have a yellow one for the mornings and a blue one for the evenings to help determine if she takes her doses of meds for each day. Every week we can load the proper amounts in each compartment and if she misses one of her doses, it will be easily noticed. I can only hope this helps.

Steph seems to be determined that she has to be able to eventually take care of herself if she is going to make it in this world in spite of her illness. And so, I am equally determined to do my part to help her attain that goal. What that will fully entail, I still have no idea. I don't think I really have a clue as to what it really means to be Bipolar 1.

We have quickly discovered it is best for her to take most of her meds late in the evening since they make her extremely sleepy. As soon as she takes those meds she gets very lethargic, which seems to be a common side affect for most people just starting these types of medications. Matt and I often jest about whether or not I have "darted her" yet, due to how rapidly she falls into a sleep/coma within twenty minutes of taking her depakote and anti-psychotic...then good luck in getting her up the next morning.

During the past several months of treatment she has switched to a number of different antidepressants looking for one that shows the most improvement. Adjusting to each of them has been a trial in itself, due to the fact that most of them take several weeks to show results. Each one has become a new hope, and then new disappointment as her depression varies from slightly better to worse. Steph frequently complains that they make her feel funny; she really hasn't been happy with any of them since they all seem to make her dopy and disoriented.

Sometimes when you're in the midst of a crisis, it can seem as if nothing else exists. It can even seem like nothing else is going on, but life doesn't really work that way. Your life and those lives of others do continue; you just aren't paying attention to anything outside of your own troubled small world. It's as if you've developed tunnel vision, only seeing what you think is important to you in your little world. Then you're taken aback when anything happens that disrupts that facade.

As I have feared, at the end of the year her father informs me that his insurance at work is changing. While she can still be covered she will again have to provide documentation showing her enrollment in school. This creates anxiety since she barely attended any of her classes this past semester. We decide to enroll her again in a full load of classes in the spring, and hope for the best. Unless something drastically changes in her condition, I know in my heart, it will just be at repeat of the last semester.

Panic sets in as we discover her doctor is not on the new insurance plan. The thought of having to see a different doctor is deeply troubling to us both, since we have come to trust and rely on his advice and treatment choices. How will the next doctor see her condition? With renewed concern over this particular issue I contemplate how my daughter's life will be in the years to come.

I really shouldn't give the impression that all is doom and gloom in our house. Some days it seems that way, but there are spells of excitement and lighthearted teasing going on just to help us all keep our sanity. We have adopted sayings to make light of the situation, such as if Steph is having a bad day we refer to her as being a loopy. On her more energetic days, we take turns sporadically running through the house singing our own made up song "it's a mania - mania day."

Phillip often just shakes his head at her antics and refers to her affectionately as his "twisted sister". He's never been much of a talker, choosing instead to keep his emotions bottled up inside himself just like his Dad. I'm sure this is also tearing him apart; seeing his sister change as drastically as she has, is most likely far beyond his understanding.

Anytime I try to talk to him about her, he just gets frustrated with me and my ramblings or completely clams up. I know he just doesn't want to talk about it and I continually have to remind myself; he probably misses her as much as I do.

Her eyes are the biggest clue in how the day is going to go; on good days they appear clearer and more focused. On bad days when depression is a main concern they seem unfocused and spacey. In the extreme, when our fears of full blown mania are at its height, they even look wild, twitching erratically. Our term for Steph's eyes when she is having one of her really bad days is "looking wiggy".

This observation in someone's eyes can easily be made in anyone's health; even those with a simple cold, you can just see it in their eyes that they don't feel well. Steph eyes, give key clues to how she feels every time her mood swings. These swings are sometimes so rapid; I get dizzy just trying to follow along.

While some may take offense to these quips, it has become a way for us to cope, right along with Steph. It doesn't bother Steph, in fact she often laughs right along with us. Unless she is totally unstable, her attitude about her illness is usually pragmatic, coupled with a tender sense of humor. She often expresses gratitude for her families open

103

participation in her treatment, and our willingness to share in her suffering. I think she counts on us to play the role of her barometer or compass to keep her on the right course.

It's really beginning to sink home that when a family member is stricken with a mental illness it not only affects that person but, the whole family. Our family dynamics has completely changed and it feels like we are all being sucked into this hopeless abyss of a nightmare right along with her. It's easy for me to see how a mental illness in a loved one can tear a family apart. The chaos it creates can be totally disrupting, even if you are trying your best to keep your emotions contained.

I often wonder what it is like to be in her shoes, not knowing what each day will bring. Despair and hopelessness takes over your mind without any control, wild crazy ideas popping into your head begging to be put into action. Not ever being able to concentrate on any one task long enough to see it to completion. Remembering yourself and what you were like before and yet knowing you will never be the same again. It's no wonder Steph doesn't usually want to get out of bed and face the challenges of her world.

Sitting on the porch after work with Matt, we are startled by the sudden ringing of the phone. The caller id identifies an unknown Florida number. Matt's father, Arthur lives in South Florida so I hand him the phone. The bits of conversation I can overhear and the concerned look on Matt's face alerts me to a new crisis. Something has happened to his father.

Though in his late seventies, Arthur lives alone, still drives his own car and pretty much does whatever he wants. Now he's has been in a car accident and is in the hospital. Although he is not considered to be critically injured, test results show a small fracture in his spine. I'm surprised to hear, in spite of this injury, he is to be released to go home in a few days.

Being a man prone to quick decisions Matt informs me "I have to go to Florida tomorrow; I'll be gone for a few weeks. Dad can't take care of himself, he says he can hardy sit up or walk." Matt continues, "I know this is not a good time, but could you come out for a few days next week?" My first thought is of course, I want to help but then an uneasiness creeps over me. Can I leave Steph at home alone for even a few days?

Matt sees the apprehension on my face and says "How about you and Steph both come out. It might do both of you some good to get away. Florida is great this time of year." Mulling this over in my mind, I realize I am continually afraid to let her out of my sight. Even a dinner out or a long shopping trip without her near me can quickly turn me into a nervous wreck. Sensing that Matt really wants me to come out, also accepting that now is not the time to cut the apron strings, I simply nod and smile.

So many things have happened during this first year since Steph's diagnosis, it's difficult to even account for them all. Most of them are difficult to explain or understand unless you were there. Some things that are just frustrating, while other scenarios that border on the bizarre.

It is telling even in her simple inability to be affectionate with any of us anymore. Oh, how I miss the warm hugs and that radiant smile of hers. Most obvious to me is the reality that Steph's day to day behavior isn't even close to the person she has exhibited for eighteen years.

With us all reunited back at home we sit on the back porch after a short morning rain, Steph comes out and sits down with us. Continuing our conversation about everything and nothing, I notice Steph staring at a puddle on the concrete left by the rain. "Look at that puddle, I wish it would dry up like all the other puddles." She says, "It's annoying, isn't it?"

As I look over to Matt with some concern, I ask her, "It's just water from the rain Honey, why is it bothering you?" Curling up tight in the chair, she continues, as if I had never said a word. "It should be dry by now, all the other puddles are gone, why not this one?" "It's like it's staying around for something, just to aggravate me," she continues "I know it is…. that's what it doing, just trying to annoy me."

Matt is as baffled as I am, by this strange conversation and asks, "Stephanie, how are you feeling today." Again Steph ignores the question, just sitting there starring down the annoying puddle. A thought comes to my mind and I quickly get up, "I'll be right back."

As I rush upstairs in search of Steph's pill container, I hear the back door open and then a minute later, slam close. Finding the yellow box in her nightstand drawer, I already know what I will discover. The past three days of meds, glaring back at me.

Returning to the porch with meds in hand, I get there just in time to see Steph frantically mopping up the last of the puddle. It was just a puddle left from the rain, yet it annoyed her, bothered and upset her so much, she had to banish it from existence. Sometimes even the smallest of behaviors, are such glaring, telling signs.

Several times now, after not taking her meds, she has come so close to a psychotic state that we thought we should admit her to the hospital. That thought though seems to freak her out even more, so only once have we actually gone through with it and only for a weekend. I feel trapped by the conflicting feelings I have over admitting her to a psych ward. I know it is necessary for some situations but I also want to protect her from that dreaded place if at all possible. I just hope I don't make her condition worse by giving in to my own fears.

I remain somewhat reassured though because, we have discovered that as soon as she gets back on her meds, she can quickly rebound. The ultra rapid cycling feature of her illness is proving to sometimes be a blessing, as much as it can be a curse. I'm beginning to realize the importance of providing a stable and calm environment for her along with close monitoring of meds. All of these things and probably a few more yet to be discovered measures seem to be crucial factors to her regaining and maintaining a measure of stability.

Since the switch of insurance Steph has changed doctors several times, trying to find another one she feels comfortable with, which we are finding is a harder challenge than imaginable. Each time she goes to a new doctor, they want to change her medication. It seems none of them are really making a big difference. But then again, Mama is constantly whispering into my subconscious, "You have to acknowledge the idea that if she isn't on the meds, she could be worse, a lot worse."

With her mind so scattered, Steph has lost several jobs due to absences and poor performance. It seems she is not able to concentrate even if she makes it to work and her classes at the community college. Her struggle to just barely function on a daily basis seems to be the most she can handle. Hoping for a career and successful life is a far beyond her realm at this point.

All throughout high school, Steph had always had an abundance of friends and yet it seems lately she has become more and more withdrawn from them, even those with whom she had become so close. True, some of them have gone off to college; others I think just need to distance themselves from what is happening to her.

Sometimes, I think she has cut off some of those relationships, to avoid dealing with the changes they might see in her. That thought breaks my heart and I wonder if she is somehow embarrassed by what's happening to her. Though on the other hand, I also have to wonder if she is even aware of the drastic changes that are so obvious to others.

Since I park in our rear entry garage, unless Steph is home when I happen to go out front, I don't see her car that often. As I walk outside to get the mail, I notice Steph car has quiet a few more conspicuous dings on all its corners. Parked a little cock-eyed, one tire is almost flat, two hub caps are missing, and the side view mirror is duck taped in place. Her poor car seems to be mirroring the battered life of my little girl.

Remembering that Steph has had several minor accidents lately, ones that thankfully didn't involve other drivers, I cringe. I've ridden with her a few times and she seems to have trouble turning corners too sharply, hitting the curb or nicking poles in parking lots. Phillip continually teases her about needing to get a car with a cattle guard on it or one with bumper pads. Returning to the house, thinking to myself, "I can't say I disagree with him."

As I set the mail on the kitchen counter, I mention how banged up Steph's car is. In the last few months, Matt and I have had many conversations about if she should be driving or not. Matt's feelings are made clear, "With all the medication she's taking, it's probably not such a good idea for her to continue driving." "It's just a matter of time till someone gets hurt."

Pondering his words over in my mind, I can't bear the thought of taking her car away from her. She has lost so much already. Taking away such a valuable piece of her independence, really the only piece she as left, it just seems cruel. Picturing having that particular conversation with her, I can see Steph taking a terrible turn for the worse. I make up my mind; I'll talk to her about the dangers of her driving and hope for the best. I don't think she can't handle another set back like loosing her ability to drive.

Maybe I'm being foolish, but a lot of what I do lately seems foolish to me. This is not the kind of life I envisioned for my tough, independent, disciplined daughter. My heart is always in turmoil over the changes I see in her, the changes that I can't seem to find a way to help repair. Sometimes, I feel like I'm even cracking from the changes I see and I miss her, the old Steph, so very much.

In addition to her being Bipolar 1, Steph's headaches and arthritis continue to plague her, yet they seem to be taking a back seat to the more dominant problem. We rarely talk about those issues, concentrating instead on getting her stable. It's funny how the most important crisis at the moment seems to always take precedence over other problems. It's just like the saying goes" the squeaky wheel, gets the oil". I can't help but wonder will this particular wheel ever get enough oil.

Sitting on the back porch has now become a sacred refuge for both Matt and I. It's a place I have always enjoy being, especially when I need a little peace. Now it's become not only a sanctuary but a private place to plot out our battle plan for fighting this new enemy. As I vent my frustration about Steph, whether she will ever be able to take care of herself, Matt interrupts, "I know this guy, Jimmy, from high school, great guy- smart- athletic- voted the most likely to succeed."

Looking over at Matt, I can clearly see the years being rolled back in his thoughts. "Jimmy graduated with honors and was given a full academic ride to one of the best universities on the east coast", Matt continues with admiration.

Then just as I'm wondering what any of this has to do with Steph, his mood changes. With sadness, Matt adds, "During his junior year, he was hit with schizophrenia, poor guy barely graduated." A million things are running through my head. Foremost, what is he trying to tell me, how does this apply to Steph? It seems Matt is waiting for that to sink in, and then he adds, "He had to be so heavily medicated, he pretty much slept all day." "It's a shame; he was such a great guy."

Well, this is depressing, is he trying to prepare me for a lifetime of Steph's misery? Seeing the look that must be on my face, Matt goes on, "Don't you see….his case is similar to Steph's?" "He was a model teen with a very hopeful future just like Stephanie." Quickly getting to the point he adds, "After a while, he was able to get on disability. ….still is." "He lives in an apartment on his own and is doing pretty well, considering what he has."

Ah ha, now I see where this is leading. Definitely not where I would hope to see Steph go, but then again, I'm not sure what other options she has. Mulling this over in my mind for a while, I begin to see Matt's point more clearly. Steph after all, hasn't been able to keep a job, continue school…. I am still afraid to leave her alone for very long.

Clearing the limp from my throat, I ask, "You think this is what Steph should do, don't you?" Matt simply replies, "Yes, I do." "That's what it's there for isn't it?" As my head nods, my mind is screaming, "No, not that!!!!" The funny thing is… doing that would make life a little easier for her; at least she won't have to worry about a job or insurance. Why then, does this proposition leave such a bad taste in my mouth?

"Okay, I'll mention it to Steph", I reply. I can't put into words why I don't feel real conviction for this idea. However seeing her dissolve and crumble as she has these last months, I feel I must offer her this option. At least this option, in my mind, would give Steph some desperately needed breathing room.

As Steph comes down the stairs, I watch her to see what mood she's in. I've waited to time my talk about filing for disability with her, when she' in a more up mood. I know in my heart it's a depressing topic in itself and should not be brought up unless she's able to really hear the idea through. Seeing her with a lighter spring to her step, her back a little straighter, I concede that today is a good day. I hesitate, not knowing really where to begin.

"Hey Steph, are you feeling okay today?" I ask. Giving me one of her newly developed, forced half smiles she replies, "yeah, today's not bad, how 'bout you?" Procrastinating, I look for a way to ease into the topic. Huh, there is no easy way; maybe I should just be blunt, like Matt. You know, just out with it…no…even I know, I have to work my way into this conversation.

Following her into the kitchen, I casually mention, "Matt told me yesterday, about a guy he knows back in Philadelphia." As Steph gets a bottle of water out of the refrigerator, with curiosity looks she up at me. I continue, "This guy, Jimmy…." And I proceed to relay the story as closely as my nervous scattered mind can recall.

Just as I get to the part about Jimmy living on his own in an apartment because he's on disability, Steph face changes. You know how it looks, the person is fairly interested in your story, and then it dawns on them that the story point is really about them.

"Maybe this is something we should think about, I mean, you wouldn't have to worry about working, you could concentrate on getting stable… without all the stress….." then as her obvious annoyance rises to a new level, I fade to silence. In my mind a panic takes over, I don't know what to say, how to give her back the good mood that I so eloquently just blew out of the water.

"Mom, I know you think this disability thing is a good idea….that you're just trying to help, but..." I can see her take a deep breath before continuing, "Wouldn't that be like giving up, like admitting defeat?" As I open my mouth Steph puts one hand up to interrupt me…"Mom, I have to find a way to live a productive life, I won't let being Bipolar destroy me."

Looking into her eyes, I can't quite figure out if she's mad or hurt by this proposition. "I won't do it; not that, you

111

can either help me or get out of my way" she says with a confidence I haven't heard in a long time.

Watching her march back upstairs, all I can think is "Well, you have to admire her spunk." I smile as I become conscious of a renewed sense of optimism from just seeing this small spark of the old Steph. Optimism is something that I sorely need, but I feel ashamed that the source of that optimism had to come from Steph. Thankfully, Steph's stubborn determination gives me a swift kick in the pants.

In the weeks that follow, I gain a new sense of hope watching Steph and her rejuvenated attitude towards her illness. Though some days she seems to be more on the ball so to speak, Steph is still far from being able to care for herself or live on her own. With that being said, I must try to keep in mind, to do as Mama always encourages us to do, to "look on the bright side". So I accept her stubbornness as a good sign. After all, up till now, all my hopes have been focused on whether she can get out of bed for more than three days in a row.

Absorbing ourselves in the reviewing of each prescription, trying to determine which one is helping, Steph makes a decision. "Since I'll probably have to change doctors sometimes, I think I'm going to have to be more in charge of what meds I take" she declares. "You know what I mean?" "When it comes down to it, I have to find a way to self manage myself."

While this frightens me a little, I completely understand the need and desire for her to be able to self manage her treatment in some way. Yet, I can not foresee the day when she is be able to be totally self managing. I think this is my most heart wrenching concern, that Steph will always need someone near her to step in, when she goes out of balance.

Her latest doctor has her on a new anti-depressant called Effexor and after only a few weeks seems to be doing more for her than any of the others she has tried so far. She has more energy and a more positive outlook than I've seen at any point since she became ill. He also wants to change her other two medications in time. He tells Steph, "I believe it's important we work together to get you stable so you can live a productive life and I think that's very possible."

In the day's that follow, I sense that this comment does more for Steph than any of the medications she has taken thus far. I think some of her despondency over the last year could be attributed to thoughts and fears that she might always be so dependant on me. Maybe, just the idea that she will always be "not quite right in the head" opened the door wider to those feelings of hopelessness and despair. Now, she seems to have hope and more confidence again.

With an arm load of Phillip's laundry, I climb the stairs to put his clothes in his room. Once again, Phillip is off to who knows where, doing who knows what. Passing their bathroom, I hear what sounds like crying, no…angry stifled screams….no maybe it is crying. I piddle around, taking my time straightening Phillip's room, waiting for Steph to come out. When she finally does, the first thing I notice is the puffiness in her eyes.

"Are you okay?" I ask, "You look a little ragged." Steph looks at me with the newly developed slight smile and replies, "I'm better now". The puzzled look I give her prompts further comment. "Shower cry" she says, with a matter of fact tone. "What does that mean," I ask.

Steph then proceeds to tell me she how she has found a way to let some of her frustrated emotions out by having, what she has labeled, a "shower cry". When she feels her emotions getting out of control, she goes into the shower and just lets herself go. Then she proudly says, "I allow myself ten minutes of self pity but, when the shower is over, so is my self pity. It's time to take a deep breath and get on with my life."

Stunned at the idea, actually at her ability to find such a cleverly innovative and beneficial form of self therapy, I just nod in agreement. Knowing she has an enormous amount of pent up feelings without an outlet, I can see how this might be a helpful release valve in her search for maintaining stability. As I go back down stairs, I can't help but smile and think out loud, "Huh, You go, girl."

It makes sense to me that no one is always in control of their own emotions. And I think it's totally understandable that someone with a mental illness has less control over their emotional state. I'm amazed that Steph has found a way in which she can consciously practice releasing and shutting off the overflow of all those emotions.

With a renewed sense of hope, Steph pushes herself more and more towards the goal of being an independent person again. We talk often about how she needs to find ways to monitor herself and the importance of actively participating in keeping herself stable. It's comforting to hear her talk about how one day she is determined to finish school and live on her own. It gives me joy and hope beyond anything I have felt in a very long time.

Perusing the internet again, we come across several articles and reports that explain how your brain can be retrained overtime. One in particular supports the belief that, when a person, specifically with Bipolar disorder, remains unstable for a long period of time, it actually is more difficult to re-stabilize them. It goes on to say how this retraining can cause them to become caught up in a pattern of being un-stable.

Just as we are getting discouraged with this news, the article takes that same premise and turns it into a positive. It goes on to say that studies also find that if a person can remain stable for a long period of time that their brain can also be re-programmed. This reprogramming, can actually give them a better chance of staying stable for longer periods of time. "Huh, this is interesting," I comment.

114

Steph is so absorbed in the article; it's as if she's no longer aware of me sitting there. It's seems nothing else in the world exists, just her and this newfound article of hope. As I continue reading, the information goes on to stress how simple lifestyle practices can make an enormous difference in ones stability. Things such as having consistent eating and sleeping schedules, regular exercise and a focus on reducing stress can be hugely beneficial. All these habits seem to show very promising results. This reinforces the idea that the more regimented and stable your lifestyle, the better chance one has in remaining mentally stable.

This is very encouraging to us, since for the most part all we have read previously about Bipolar 1, seem to be negative, doom and despair. Up until now most of what we have experienced personally with Steph and this illness has leaned strongly toward those definitions. This all makes very practical sense to us, but trying to implement it as a part of Steph's routine is another matter all together. As a new power struggle begins, Steph makes it clear, she needs the Momma Bear to let go, just a little. But I know in my heart, this will prove, to be easier said than done.

In the weeks that follow as I try to force myself to let go a little, Steph begins to take on a new attitude about her illness and seems to be making great strides in her own self management. I begin to try and relax more and let my focus drift back to other aspects of the household that I have neglected since her diagnosis.

Frustration has run high with everyone this past year or so and I just haven't had the energy or time to notice. Now that my head is out of the fog, I can see that Phillip has been sorely overlooked. He is more withdrawn and moody than ever and is hanging out with a different group of kids. While his room has always been a struggle to keep clean, it now always looks like a tornado hit it. It's becoming a challenge just to get him to bathe and put on clean clothes.

115

Phillip is failing almost all of his classes again this year and now he wants to drop out of school and try to get his G.E.D. Discussing it with Matt, we agree that maybe this isn't such a bad idea given his academic abilities. As we finally agree to sign off on it, I can't help but wonder what will be come of him and his future.

As the months go by Phillip becomes more and more withdrawn. Matt tells me, "I think he's just depressed." Hearing those words send me into a panic terrified state. What if my second child has the same problem as the first child? What does any mother do when faced with this thought? I make an appointment with Steph's doctor. If Phillip is Bipolar; I want to know right away.

Well, Phillip is none to happy about going to see "a shrink". He bluntly tells me, "I'm not crazy." I want to believe he's okay but I am on a mission to get to the bottom of this before it gets too far out of control. My mind is full of the fear that he is also Bipolar. I'm scared to death that we will have to go through the last few years of turbulent chaos, again. Holding firm to the appointment, we leave for the doctor; Phillip fuming all the way.

After an hour of consultation, the doctor pulls me in a room privately and tells me "Philip definitely is not Bipolar. He is behaving like any teenager would when their mother has been so preoccupied for the last few years." I feel terrible realizing that I have spent all my time and energy focused on Steph and her problems.

It's not a pleasant feeling, acknowledging that I have left Phillip out in the cold. Now that I think about it, I can see that he has been trying to deal with his last few teen years on his own. I'm sure it hasn't been easy either, seeing his sister go through this crisis. Feeling frustrated and all alone, he has had no one to turn to but other teens, apparently other mixed up teens. Though I am relieved by the confirmation that he's not Bipolar, I'm also devastated that I have failed him so miserably.

During the ride home we talk more about him than we have in a long time. Most of the interaction we have had over the last few years has been about Steph, and I realize how much I have neglected him. But one of the wonderful things about Phillip is how forgiving he can be. He just smiles and says, "Its okay Mom, I know you've had a lot on your mind." As I vow to make amends, I know in my heart I must find the energy and time to be more involved in his life.

It's been over a year now, since Matt and I began living together and we continue to get along well for the most part, considering the stress we are under. I have become accustom to him being my sounding board and my soft place to fall. I can always count on him to allow me to fall apart, patiently talk me through my inner turmoil and then help me put myself back together again. I hold him thoroughly responsible, for giving me the ability to be there for Steph, when she needs me the most.

Steph has taken many different anti-depressant medications since her diagnosis which include Wellbutrin, Paxil, Celexa, Nortriptyline and now finally Effexor, all in varying combinations and strengths. There are probably a few others I fail to remember. Steph's depression is more under control with the latest antidepressant switch and her doctor decides it's time to make a few other changes in her other meds. I'm not disappointed to hear that he thinks its time to take her off the Depakote and try some other medications to better stabilize her mood and psychotic episodes.

It continues to amaze me, how each person responds so differently to each of these medications. Steph's doctor reminds us, "It can't be stressed enough, what works for one may not work for another." "It is crucial that we encourage our loved ones to keep searching for that best mix that gives them the greatest measure of relief and stability."

This search seems to be one of the biggest problems for those with mental illnesses. Often during this search, they are not able to see any light at the end of the tunnel, and have the tendency to give into despair. So it seems it's up to the support team to keep the hope alive of finding relief from the torment of mental illnesses. I have come to believe this is one of our most essential duties.

And being aware, that this is one of the biggest concerns for Steph, I'm obsessed with it. I'm always fretting over whether or not she is taking her meds—and if those meds are doing the trick. But it seems like every time I let go a little and allow her to handle it on her own, she goes off her meds. As soon as I detect something is amiss, I quickly have to scoop her back up and take over for a few days, until she regains her stability. I feel like a sheep dog, herding my lost little lamb back into the fold.

Thankfully she responds quickly to her meds and a reassuring stable environment. The calmer her surroundings, the easier it is for her to return to stability again. It's plain to see that being on her meds is a vital part the key. However, I'm also beginning to see that there is more to the treatment of being Bipolar, than just taking some meds.

It's getting easier for me to tell when she goes off her meds; she either has a wild look about her and her thought process becomes completely haywire. Or, I'll notice that she either sleeps for days or does not sleep at all for days. If all else fails I can just look at her check register. The scribbles and missing information is always a telling sign.

Sometimes it's so obvious to us that we have a difficult time understanding how Steph fails to see the importance of taking her medication. But then again this very point is what makes this disorder so difficult to treat.

It is a never ending battle, the taking or not taking of meds that is also reported to be a symptom of this disorder. It seems that all people with Bipolar typically have this difficulty. They think they no longer need their meds to function, instead of understanding that it's the meds that are keeping them functioning. It continues to be true, even if they are able to find the right mix that works for them. It's a vicious circle of tricks their mind plays on them, that many never find a way to cope with. Many of them instead turn in desperation to, alcohol or illegal drugs to ease their pain.

As the weeks and months fly by, we continue through cycles of Steph doing well for a few weeks, then something strange happens and we quickly discover that she's off her meds yet again. We begin to refer to this as her being out of balance and I have to get her back on her meds. Each time she quickly rebounds back and continues on her way.

These spells, when she is off her meds, are often riddled with mini crisis such as a car accident, an overdrawn bank account or a lost job. A few times she has to be taken to the hospital after fainting or blacking out. Even after seeing the doctor, we still don't have a concrete cause for such type of episodes, other than possible side effects from her meds.

I would have to say; to me this is one of the most difficult parts of having a child with this illness. There is such a fine line between assisting her self management and my wanting to take over completely. Often we get into arguments about it and I wonder if our lives will forever revolve around this continuous struggle between us.

I also wonder sometimes if I am crazy in hoping that she can ever be successful in any form of self management. Even if we find the right meds, will I ever be able to relax my grip? Knowing me, I probably won't. The Momma Bear always reigns supreme.

What am I doing during this time; that is, myself? As emotionally, physically and mentally exhausted as I am in the midst of this turmoil, I simply am trying to survive, to maintain my own sanity.

Though I seem to avoid the phrase "it could be worse", I am just trying to do as Mama taught me. Daily fighting to just keep moving... keep putting one foot in front of the other....keep my focus on someone else so I don't fall apart. But mostly, I am hoping and praying, very fervently I might add, that "this too shall pass"

CHAPTER 8   Summer 2001

Each set back is traumatic for me as well as Steph, reminding us both that her mental stability and her daily struggles with life are so very fragile. Yet each time, she gets back on her meds and renews her push forward in another attempt to find some level of independence. She reminds us, of that famous "energizer bunny" on T.V.; no matter what happens to her "she's still going."

I am beginning to see some sparks of the old Steph and with a renewed hope we push forward. She has found a good job with a property management company that offers good benefits and pays her fairly well. Things are starting to look up for her, though it is a very long winding hill to climb.

Amazingly, during the first year or so of her illness she and I have been able to pay the minimum on each of her credit cards and now with more money coming in each week she begins to make larger payments in the hope of paying them off. Her ability to focus on dealing with day to day issues is showing considerable improvements.

With her new job and financial situation improving, Steph decides to purchase a new car. She definitely needs one since her old car is so beat up. I am proud to see that she is in a practical mind and selects one that is affordable as well as boasts of good gas mileage. Though I have to co-sign for her, she has enough to make her own down payment and we talk them into a good interest rate. Traces of the old Steph are slowly but surely beginning to shine through.

With things improving for Steph, I begin to relax slightly and focus a little more on other issues in our home. Phillip has somehow completed his night classes and recently passed his G.E.D. test. While I am happy he has accomplished this, I am still concerned over his behavior and attitude. His future looks bleak, and he seems to be spiraling further and further into his own world. We are constantly arguing about how late he stays out at night and him sleeping most of the day. As he quickly loses his second job, I'm not really shocked, but find myself continually frustrated.

Much of the time Matt and I spend on the porch is now spent talking about what Phillip should be doing. Though we are in agreement about him finding another job and being more productive, I always seem to feel compelled to defend him. Even though this scenario plays out a little too often, I allow his laziness to continue for months. When I discover that he is involved in drugs, I crumble. Staring in the face of this new crisis, I can't help but think, "I must be blind, not to see this coming!"

I don't mean to give the impression that he is a raging drug addict but he is regularly smoking pot and probably experimenting with other drugs as well. Studies have shown that marijuana typically makes people lazy and lethargic. That attitude of not caring what happens to you from day to day is very self evident in Phillip. While there are many other concerns regarding the use of pot and its effects, our main concern where this will lead and that it is hindering him from being motivated in his search for a job and finding a general direction his life.

While I appreciate that Matt has been very instrumental in supporting me with Steph since her diagnosis, the pressure I feel from him, to nip this new crisis in the bud seems to be pushing me further in the opposite direction. In my mind, I can see where the old problem of focusing my efforts on defending my loved one is taking precedence over my ability to see what needs to be done. I know I'm doing this, in part due to the enormous guilt I feel for not paying closer attention to Phillip, since Steph became ill. I just can't seem to stop myself.

I also understand that stepparents are in a difficult position when it comes to discipline, especially when it comes to almost grown children. While I understand Matt's feelings, that he should have an equal say in our household, I also firmly believe that I, being the parent, should be the one to enforce the discipline.

But what is it about me, that make's me feel like I have to defend Phillip's actions instead of insisting he do the right thing? I keep making excuses for him and his irresponsible behavior that he doesn't deserve. I also know this is probably not an uncommon problem in the adjustment of parents and stepparents. I just can't seem to find the ability to remain frustrated with Phillip and his actions. I'm too busy letting myself be aggravated by Matt's complaints.

As the weeks pass, as well as many arguments, I finally think I have made it clear enough to Matt, that in order for me to deal with the problem at hand, I need him to only support me and my discipline enforcement tactics. Our most recent discussion has left us with a truce. Matt promises to not comment on Phillip's behavior and I promise to start putting my foot down.

I'm not at all confident, I can be the tough love kind of Mom that Phillip apparently needs. Thinking about how I've reacted in the past, shows me that I haven't always dealt properly with the reality of the situation. But, as I think of the difference in my children and their needs, I remember that Phillip is not mentally ill as Steph is. Pondering on this and the challenges that Steph has faced, makes me recognize that she didn't always have control. Phillip does and he's consciously making the wrong choices. In a way, this realization gives me a new kind of determination to see this through.

With Matt keeping his word and being quieter, it is now time for me to live up to my end of the bargain. As I climb the stair, my nerves are on edge, it's too quiet. Knocking several times on Phillips door, I'm thinking about what to say to him. Finally turning the knob, seeing him sound asleep at six in the evening again, makes something in me snap.

Finding a glass in the bathroom, I fill it with water and return to Phillips room. I take a deep breath and toss the wake up call in his face. I' m surprised by the calm that has come over me, as he startles awake, sputtering and shaking his head. Remembering his childhood, facing the numerous mini crisis that come with raising children, I recognize the calmness that a parent feels when they finally do the right thing.

As I begin to set and enforce strict guidelines for Phillip, things quickly fall apart. As soon as I confront Phillip about his drug use, he turns more sullen and resentful. But I've finally made up my mind. I stand firm and tell him, "Under no circumstances can you live in our house and continue to use drugs and sleep all day." "Phillip, you must stop this nonsense and get a job." By default, he chooses drugs and laziness and I have to ask him to leave. It is one of the most difficult things, I have ever had to say to him and my heart breaks. Matt again, becomes my soft place to fall.

After two weeks of roaming from one friend's house to another, Phillip pleads to come home. I'm excited to see him but know that I must remain firm if tough love is to have a chance. "Our rules have not changed but you are always welcome to live with us under those rules," I state hoping the nervousness I feel is not giving me away.

Waiting for his answer, it seems as if my little boy is struggling with the decision of his life. Maybe he is....and my heart leaps for joy as he agrees to the terms. As I watch him carry his bag upstairs, defeated and heavy hearted, a sense of renewed hope stirs within me. Phillip turns around at the top of the stairs and asks, "Mom, can you make sure I wake up in the morning, so I can go look for a job." Never being one to hold a grudge, with a slight smile on his face, he continues, "Even if you have to throw water on me?"

In the weeks that follow, Phillip gets up each day and looks for a job. But he has no particular skill, a poor work history and it proves to be a difficult task for him. I can see him getting frustrated. I feel awful for Phillip. Even though I believe he has given up his drugs, I know it will be difficult for him to find a job, at least, one that will lead to any real success in his life.

Since he has done poorly in school and doesn't have any specific training in anything; he has no idea how he is going to make a living. The tension is clear on his face. Once again, Matt proves to be a driving force in our family. It seems he is always running to someone's rescue.

A week later, breezing through the kitchen, Matt passes me and calls upstairs, "Phillip, hey Phillip, get down here." He had left early this morning to get his oil changed and now, I can see that something has excited him. He definitely looks like a man on a happy mission. As Phillip nervously bounds down the stairs, "I'm up... I'm going to the mall again..." he stammers. "Forget that, you need to go to Kwik Car right now" Matt declares. "You just might have a job."

I don't know who's more stunned and confused... me or Phillip. While getting his oil changed, Matt took it upon himself to persuade the owner of the shop to give Phillip a chance to work for them. He explained to the owner that although Phillip has no real experience in this field, he is very good with most mechanical things. His persistency paid off, he was told to send Phillip over for an interview that same day.

Later that afternoon, Phillip is shocked and thrilled to be starting as, what he considers to be a cool new job, an oil change technician. We can see the relief plainly on his face. A face that for the past few years has bore the strain of a teen with no idea what he is going to do with his life. Not so long ago, I sat with him in his room, watching tears roll down his eyes as he contemplated his future job possibilities. As the weeks pass, I'm thrilled to see him arrive home each day with grease all over him and something I haven't seen in a long time: a big smile on his face.

In the whole scheme of things, this period of crisis with Phillip hasn't been so bad. He could have very easily traveled much farther down the road to self destruction. While I'm still not convinced his future is, by any means secure, I do find joy in the fact that he's healthy and happy in his life. And isn't this suppose to be the main goal of what parenting is all about; directing and guiding your child towards finding his own way in the world?

As a parent, I am beginning to see another one of my failings. I haven't taught Phillip how to keep putting one foot in front of the other and to remember that things could be worse. I haven't stressed to him the wise words of wisdom I learned from Mama, which I know can give hope and encouragement in tough times. But I am so thankful that at least it seems in this particular situation, "this too has passed".

While Phillip is beginning to succeed in his endeavors, Steph is also progressing forward. Yes, she still periodically misses work due to her migraines and nausea from her medications but her new supervisor seems to be sympathetic to her plight. Steph has made her aware of her mental illness and the need for her frequent doctor appointments. Though I have some concern about being this open, Steph asserts that she will always be up front and matter of fact about her illness.

It seems the more stable Steph is the more confident she becomes with the mindset that her illness is just another illness. No, she's not belittling being Bipolar, she's just looking at it from a pragmatic view. She feels, for her to succeed in this world she needs to accept her illness just as directly as a person with diabetes or any other form of a disability. She doesn't seem to want to seek sympathy or special treatment, and her determination to live an independent life intensifies.

Steph seems to be more stable now than at any point since her illness began and after months of working in her new position she wants to move into her own apartment. Of course I'm panicked. The thought of not having access to the day to day monitoring scares me out of my mind. Yes, she is doing well, but will she continue to progress if she is left to her own caretaking?

The next few months Steph spends her time dreaming of her own apartment and purchasing some of the many things needed to start a household. Throughout her teenage years she had already accumulated a wide array of household items ranging from a toaster, a can opener, towels and dishes. Now she is in search of larger items such as a vacuum cleaner, microwave and even some furniture. We watch apprehensively as each week, our upstairs living area becomes filled with items that will soon be taken to her new apartment.

Muddled in somehow with all the chaos during the past few years, Matt and I have come to the conclusion that we are a perfect fit and so, we decide to get married. We have a small ceremony in our home with only immediate family attending. The difficulties of the past few years have convinced us that if we could make it through that, we can endure anything else thrown our way. The ability to rely on each others strengths rank right up there with the comforting love that has grown between us.

As Matt and I begin our life together as husband and wife, Steph stays focused on her endeavor to live on her own. She also becomes focused on finding a better paying job. I'm a little nervous about the idea, since her current employer seems to be very understanding of her illness and frequent absences. I can't help but think, shouldn't we leave well enough alone.

Piddling around in the kitchen with Steph, I ask, "Why do you want to change jobs so bad?" It seems to me that she's almost afraid to tell me something. "What, what is it?" I persist. As she squares her shoulders and takes a deep breath, she says, "I'm afraid my manager is getting tired of having to cover for my absences." Since being fired is now a familiar experience for her, she has decided to find a new job before that day comes to pass.

The following Saturday while getting her hair cut, Steph mentions to her hairdresser that she is looking for a new job. The hairdresser tells her of another regular customer she has, that is looking for an administrative assistant and she thinks he would be very impressed with her. After getting the man's number, she calls him the next Monday morning, and sets up an interview. A few weeks later Steph starts a new administrative assistant position making more money than she ever anticipated.

While this sounds very exciting, I must admit I'm even more anxious, frantically worrying that her new found financial success will enable her to move out on her own. I know this is her goal, but I'm not sure my nerves can handle her being out of my care. Yes, she is progressing well, taking her meds on her own regularly, eating and sleeping well, but will that continue? If she goes off her meds and regresses back into instability, how will I know? The possibilities and dangers that can easily unfold before I am able to intervene are endless.

In a desperate attempt to control the situation, I find myself constantly arguing with Steph. Who am I kidding...... I'm even arguing with myself lately. It's just not that easy for me to accept that I will not have any ability to monitor her daily life and it's terrifying to me. I'm so fearful she'll go off her meds and become unstable. Even more afraid she will return to that mental place she was not so very long ago, curled up in the corner of her room, twitching, looking wildly off... into nothingness..... No matter what she says to reassure me, I can't get that picture out of my mind.

I have to admit though, that a part of me is proud, proud of the young lady that seems so determined to take charge of her life in spite of her illness. A much bigger part of me though knows the day may never come when I can relax. I just can't see her on her own. I have become so ingrained with the mindset that I'm her sole support and that I must always be available to her. I have only recently become able to go a few hours at a time each day, without being so consumed with her mental health.

As I vent my frustration and worry about Steph moving out, Phillip, in his simplistic way says "Mom, you always told us we need to learn to stand on our own two feet." Noting that I'm really listening, he continues, "And that we should never give up; that there is a way to fix anything. Isn't that what you're wanting Steph to do.......give up?" Thinking about his words and the sincerity behind them, I realize.....It's my own words coming back to haunt me.

Each time Matt and I have a conversation about Steph moving out, it ends with me crying, frustrated by the very thought of her living on her own. Though Matt always proclaims, "she needs to at least try to live on her own, for her own peace of mind." His proclamation is always followed by, "I do agree that she may never be able to be totally independent, but it's important for her to make the attempt....important for both of you."

It's difficult for me to find any solace in her need to make the attempt, since I know the worse case scenario is one I'm not willing to face. A much more serious risk is at stake; a risk even more serious than the regressing back into that old familiar instability. A risk I can't seem to even allow myself to put into words.

Though I know in my heart, I have to let Steph at least try to live on her own, even need to give her my support and encouragement, I also know in my heart, her illness will fight her every step of the way. No matter how much the old Steph will try to battle this beast into submission, I know the new Steph will often find herself overwhelmed with a power beyond her control. It seems to me, the word control will always be at the center of what I fear the most.

After researching many apartments, comparing prices and location, Steph puts her deposits down on an apartment. Though it's nice and safe, I think it's a little too expensive for her. With years under my belt of paying bills and trying to live within my own means, I know how often a self imposed budget can come up short. Seeing your budget on paper never seems to play out the same as it does in the realities of the day to day living. Something always comes up that's not planned for.

As Steph prepares to move in, her current boyfriend, John, begins discussing moving in with her. A part of me, wishes he would. In theory, he could help her pay the bills and help me, monitor her mental health. But his recent history doesn't give me much hope in this theory, since he currently is unemployed and hanging out with friends seems a little too important to him. I also have some suspicions that he is on some sort of drugs though I don't really know why.

It seems that I always need something to worry about but, my mind is quickly put to rest on this issue. It isn't long before, Steph tells John that since he doesn't have a job, he can't live with her and they break up. Steph also confirms to me that he has been using drugs and that is the main reason for breaking up with him.

While her living alone makes me very nervous, I'm glad she is adhering to such reasonable principles. I can see where John would have been perfectly happy to stay there for months upon endless months "getting stoned" while she supports them both. That is not the kind of situation I want her involved in.

It's not that I think he is such a bad guy; John just seems to be one of those young men who have no direction, motivation or desire to make something of his life. It seems to me since she became ill; these are frequently the kind of young men Steph chooses to date. I have come to believe, it is indicative of the way she feels about herself; as if she is saying to herself, I'm not good enough to date a better quality of young man.

Moving day arrives with a flurry of excitement and I sadly help her set up her apartment. While she is thrilled and giddy, I'm having a difficult time finding any sense of happiness for her. My nerves are raw because deep inside my heart I know this will not pan out as she thinks, but feel powerless to stop it.

As the first few weeks roll by, we talk every day and I feel a measure of pride that my little girl seems to be making it on her own just fine. Steph assures me, each time I ask, that she is taking her medication daily and is feeling fine. I know that I'm probably annoying her to no end, with all my questions and phone calls. I continue to struggle in my effort to not feel so consumed with worry. I can't help privately picturing the many frightening scenarios that can play out.

Without Steph living at home, the tension of the last few years slowly begins to melt away and I try to start living my own life again. I somehow discover that I can enjoy playing a round of golf with Matt without worrying about being gone too long. Amazingly, I can even carry on a conversation without Bipolar becoming the main topic. Yet that doesn't change the fact that Steph and her illness are never far from my mind.

It reminds me of those years after my divorce when Steph and Phillip were little and I returned to the work force, after many years of being a stay at home mom. Just like being

131

a new mother can be all consuming; it seems I have been so consumed by Steph's illness that I have become isolated and ignorant of what's going on in the outside world, even my own.

How is it possible that I have continued to work and even advance in my position while all this has been going on and not really have any remembrance of those day to day events? Somehow, those words of persuasion to keep putting one foot in front of the other must have pressed me on without my full awareness. God bless my Mama.

The next few months or so pass with a few minor occurrences, just simple ones such as "Mom, I'm a little short on my electric bill" or "Mom, my insurance is due and I don't get paid until Friday". These all seem trivial in the whole scheme of things and I of course help out. Frankly, I'm relieved and surprised that thus far, nothing more detrimental has occurred. Sometimes, I think I even miss being needed so much.

During a phone conversation, Steph tells me that she has been dating a few new young men, employed and drug free young men I'm happy to add. With her confidence on the rise apparently so are other aspects of her life. Then rather quickly something begins to change; each time she stops by to see us, we notice fancy new clothes, shoes and it isn't long before she shows up in another new more expensive car.

While some parents would be pleased to see their daughter doing so well, Matt and I are apprehensive. Her attitude, when we mention the concern of added expenses to an already tight budget, is flippantly dismissive. As Matt and I discuss the changes, I find myself defending Steph from his accusations of being a little too cocky and snobbish. Even with alarm bells ringing loudly in my head, I somehow find a way to close my eyes to the reality. I know I'm being foolish but, I just don't want to face the possibility that anything is wrong.

Over the next week or so I find I have difficulty reaching Steph on the phone. The few times I do get her to answer; she is distant and impatient with my queries about what's going on with her and seems to be always in such a rush to hang up. The bells are ringing as loud as Saint Peter's Cathedral and I know something is going on even as she assures me she's fine. A Momma Bear always knows; we can just hear it in their voice when something is amiss.

A few weeks later Steph calls me and ask, "Mom can you stop by my apartment on your way home from work?" I know something is wrong just from the request but also by the shakiness in her voice. As I enter her apartment, my suspicions are confirmed by the look on her face. Steph quickly admits that she has gone off her meds and can't seem to balance her checkbook. First things first, I insist we sit down, refill her med dispensers and take her dose of meds for the day. Then I ask, "Let's look at your checkbook and see if we can figure out what's going on with your bank account."

Once again her check book looks as if a first grader has taken over, scribbles and missing information everywhere. Several hours later, we come to the conclusion that she will have at least a dozen overdraft fees. In spite of the pay check she is holding in her hand, Steph still will be short over two hundred dollars on her rent that was due two days ago. I try not to cringe as I agree to help her get caught up if she gives me the reassurance that she will religiously take her meds.

As I've said before, this is one of the primary evils with this disorder, the failure to take the meds needed. While this particular episode has not driven her to the deepest pits of despair as it had before, it has allowed the other just as feared aspect to manifest itself, mania. Though this scenario seems bad, as Mama has always said, it could be worse. Thankfully, it has not gone too far out of control this time, before reining her back in. Still, the voice in my head is still whispering, no, I should say screaming, she can't do this on her own.

Wanting to keep her in check over the next month or so proves to be more and more difficult as she continues to avoid my calls. She is rarely home when I stop by her apartment. On the few occasions that I reach her on the phone, Steph quickly says she is fine and makes excuses to hang up. The bells and whistles are going off piercingly in my head but short of kidnapping her there seems to be little I can do. Believe me; I actually am considering doing just that.

Another few weeks pass and I receive a tearful phone call from Steph. She has been in an accident in her new car. While driving to meet someone for lunch, she comes upon a stalled car in the middle lane of a main road. She didn't see the stalled car until the car in front of her changes lanes. With such little time, she didn't react fast enough and she ran into the stalled car. Both cars are completely wrecked. Fortunately, the other driver was standing on the curb making a phone call for help when she hits his car and is not hurt. Steph luckily only has a few minor injuries needing medical attention but she is still pretty shook up about the incident.

With her new car now totally destroyed, Steph has difficulty the next few days finding rides to work and to her physical therapy appointments needed for her neck & shoulder injury. I'm helping as much as I can but my job is thirty minutes away in the opposite direction. I can sense her frustration rising as she struggles to work out the many details and complications the accident has caused.

Life events are sometimes fully within our control and yet there are others that are merely the results of our misguided choices or even lack of choice. It seems to me, these choices shape a huge portion of our lives, if not all of it. Looking back, I can see how Steph's life lately, has been riddled with more than her fair share of frustration and chaos. Though I must admit, much of her pain has been created by her own actions or lack of action. It's exasperating to watch and sometimes even foresee how these deeds and misdeeds reshape her life in a way that I never imagined.

CHAPTER 9 Spring 2002

As I hang up the phone a few days later, my mind is flooded with the possible devastating outcomes of the latest news. Steph has just told me that she has not paid her car insurance this past month and her agent just informed her that her policy was canceled two days before the accident. Not only would her car not be repaired or replaced, but the other car's owner and insurance company would most likely come after her personally for their damages. In addition, all her automobile accident injury related medical visits will not be covered.

While this is not the end of the world, while you're in the middle of this type of situation it certainly can seem so. The stress and worry quickly set Steph off on another series of emotionally unstable episodes. It seems that she is having great difficulty concentrating on her duties at work and often calls me in tears. In the middle of the day at the end of the next week she calls me crying uncontrollably. It takes me several minutes to understand that what she is asking me to do is to pick her up; she has been fired.

Just from hearing her talk, as I take her home I realize she is off her meds again. Understandably, she is upset over losing her job, but her behavior seems much more erratic than normally would be expected. As she explains why she was fired, it doesn't make any sense, babbling almost incoherently, something about her co-workers. It's just like when someone has the flu; you can see something wrong in their eyes. Steph's eye's are definitely telling, with a wildness that I've come to know all too well. I walk up to her apartment with her to make sure first and foremost, she takes her medicine.

We sit down and look over her scribbled checkbook and stack of unpaid bills. With her now out of work, there is no decision left to make, she needs to move back home. It seems to bring a measure of relief to Steph, as I begin to make plans to move her back home over the weekend.

The next morning we rent a truck, put her furniture in storage and move her back home. While I'm relieved to have her back under a more stable and controlled environment, I'm also not looking forward to the continual disruption that comes with her illness. I have come to realize this is a daily struggle I will have to learn to cope with in order to keep my commitment to try and be her rock.

Throughout the next week, I insist on taking charge of giving Steph her meds each morning and night. I know that the best way to get her stable is to insure her meds are taken and then encourage her in the search for a new job. Seeing her curl up into a ball each day tells me her mental state is very fragile. As I watch her struggle in this way, I try to keep my own sanity by telling myself, "It could be worse and this too shall pass." I believe keeping an upbeat attitude around the house is crucial in preventing her depression from completely taking over.

At the end of the next week, I go to the pharmacy to pick up her refills on her meds. The pharmacy clerk returns after a few minutes and says, "I'm sorry, this insurance policy is coming back on the computer as canceled, is there another policy in effect?"

For a moment, I stand there puzzled, and then I realize Steph's company must have canceled it at the end of the month. I don't see this as a big problem since her Dad also has Steph covered on his plan. So I reply, "Oh, yes I forgot, please rerun the prescriptions under her Dad's plan number." I give her his insurance card I keep in my purse and step back to wait for the refills again. To my horror, I'm informed that this card was also canceled a few months ago.

I stand there feeling at least as foolish as I'm sure I must look. Quickly, I mentally run through what my available balances on my credit cards should be. I know each of the medications are expensive but am totally taken aback when I'm told the total amount for all three prescriptions are a little more than six hundred dollars. I don't see another choice other than to pay for them with two of my credit cards. I drive home in a fog, thinking about what this added expense will mean to us in the next few months. Is it my imagination or wasn't there a country western song, year's ago that sang the phrase "Stop the world and let me off"?

As soon as I get home, I call Steph's dad. Mike tells me he had canceled her coverage on his plan because Steph had told him she had a job with benefits and didn't need the plan anymore. I can't help but think to myself, I wish he had discussed this with me first, but what can I do now? He feels terrible and agrees to add her back on his plan during the next open enrollment. Unfortunately, that will be several months away.

Along with the meds she will need each month; we will also have to pay for her monthly psychiatrist appointment. All these expenses will continue until she is either placed back on her dad's insurance or finds another job with medical benefits. As I ponder on this thought, I force myself to repeat like a mantra, Mama's phrases, "it could be worse, just keep putting one foot in front of the other." Mostly, I pray that......"this too shall pass."

Frantically, trying to work out the details of paying for more than seven hundred dollars a month, I'm quickly frustrated. This just covers her mental health; I can't even think about her other monthly bills or the replacement of her car. Along with his continued moral support, Matt, seeing the impossible task at hand, assures me that he can help cover of the cost. What would I ever do without him?

As we settle back into our old familiar routine, I again fight the feelings of fear, anger, frustration and overwhelming sadness. I so often find myself asking the "why" question, as I struggle to discover a way to accept and cope with the helplessness and frustration I feel, as I watch the effects this illness has on my daughter.

I see her, as someone that has fallen into a dark deep cavern. Battered and bruised from the fall, all I can do is watch each day as she fights to climb up, rising a few feet only to slip and slide farther back down, as the wall crumbles in her hands. With no light, hurt and all alone, all she has is my faint voice desperately calling her from above encouraging her to never give up. I want so badly to be able to reach in and pull her out. But that scenario can never be a reality, even in my imagined scene.

I'm sure all parents struggle with this dilemma, though hopefully for them on a smaller scale. We all feel helpless sometimes, as we watch our children struggle with trials and growing pains as they find their way in this world. It seems to me, one of the most difficult duties of a parent, is to find that fine line of only guiding and directing.

Instead we often feel the urge to take completely over, in an attempt to solve all their problems. I know I often make the mistake of doing too much for my children, only reinforcing their dependence on me. I fear in Steph's case, this will forever be one of my greatest struggles. Her mental illnesses constantly makes it feel as if the line is always moving; each time, as I struggle to adjust to the difficulties as they arise, the line moves yet again.

During this past year, Phillip has continued to work at the small oil change shop, learning a wide range of skills in the vocation of automotive repairs. Feeling very secure in this knowledge and eager to learn more, he secretly applies for a full mechanic position at a large dealership. Bursting and yelling through the front door.....living room...kitchen....the back porch, Phillip's animation brings a stir of excitement.

138

"Mom, Mom, Matt, Mom!" he yells, "I got a new job!" Seeing him standing there, all aglow and full of pride, I find myself dumbfounded, as I listen to his latest adventure.

Where did this new initiative and self assuredness come from? The answer quickly comes to my mind from a lifetime of memories of Daddy…encouraging, "It feels better when you learn to do things yourself." Smiling within and outwardly to Phillip, I can't help but appreciate seeing such feelings of accomplishment in my son. His struggles of the past have quickly dissolved into an abundance of pride and a new found confidence.

He often has friends' cars in our garage doing work for them on the side and though he periodically needs help waking up in the morning, for the most part he is progressing extremely well. I've spent years, worrying about Phillip's future and his ability to take care of himself financially. It seems strange to me that things haven't turned out as I imagined.

The previous decade, I was so certain one of my children would be a success, while the other would struggle just to survive. Slowly over the past few years, I've watched one being crumbled to her knees while the other is learning to rise to new heights. The overwhelming gloomy shadow of one child is being chased away by the emerging brightness of the other and with it; a mixture of conflicting emotions falls over me.

Over the next month, Steph has difficulty finding a job from, what seems to be, primarily due to her lack of a car. Yes, some days she barely makes it out of bed but, the ability to find rides to interviews is proving to only complicate things even more. Matt and I decide we will spend three thousand dollars and buy her a used car. We both feel that it is important for her to work, to help her reestablish emotional stability. Now the search is on for something that not only is in our price range but, one that also runs.

139

We turn to Phillip for his new found expertise in cars. This not only helps us a great deal but being the "go to guy" gives him a new sense of pride. He spends the next week looking over, what he considers to be acceptable cars. As the week comes to an end, he gives us the verdict. Though the late model economy car is quite a step down for Steph, she is relieved and thankful to be back on the road again.

The following week, Steph's Dad calls with some wonderful news. He has re-enrolled her on his health plan. Mike tells me, Steph will be covered at the end of the month and agrees will not remove her without talking to me first. Things are slowly starting to look up, or well, at the least not looking down. After all we have been through I'm happy to settle for moving forward.

In the next few weeks, Steph still has trouble finding a job and this pushes her further into depression as she struggles with feelings of worthlessness and hopelessness. It's all I can do to keep her moving from day to day in a frantic attempt to not let her fall into another deep pit of despair.

With all that has been going on, I somehow have failed to notice that Steph has lost a considerable amount of weight. Matt, being only slightly less consumed with her mental health than I have been, notices how thin she has become and brings it to my attention. Guilt and feelings of maternal failure play havoc on my nerves, as I struggle to widen my scope of duties. Sometimes, it feels like I'm swimming up river in a raging rapid of ever changing events, rocks and limbs everywhere that desperately need to be avoided.

Somehow the fact that her clothes hang on her and her hair is dull, even failing out in long strands, I have failed to notice. How is it possible that I've not recognized the threat of an eating disorder again? I'm so consumed with her mental illness; I have completely missed her deteriorating physical appearance. What's wrong with me? I know good health in a person is all connected; mental to the physical and vise versa. I could just kick myself over the reality that Steph's physical health is equally important to her continual mental health.

So putting my frustration aside, we make a plan of attack, new guidelines for Steph to live by. I have decided to only require two things of her, no more use of laxatives (apparently a popular choice among young ladies) and she will have to weight in front of me every week. Since she's 5' 6' the weight I think she looks the healthiest at is around 125 lbs. Since she has already dropped to 102 lbs, we agree that she should not be less than 104 lbs. If she, at any time goes under this weight, she has a week to increase her weight above that limit. If she fails to increase her weight to that lowest limit, I will have her admitted to the hospital.

Then after maintaining her weight above 104 lbs or more for a period of two weeks we will move the lowest limit up to 108 lbs. It seems to me, that this gradual plan, will give her time to slowly gain weight up to the next limit. Then each month we could move her weight limit up slowly, until she reaches 125 lbs. I hope keeping the focus on an actual weight number will take her focus off how she looks.

I've read that, how a person who struggles with anorexia or bulimia sees themselves is apparently grossly distorted. While we all can plainly see that they are way to thin, they only see themselves as a revolting fat person. How that's possible, I'll never understand. It's true, as they say, until you walk in someone else's shoes you just can't comprehend, only do your best to empathize.

No.....understanding is definitely beyond my ability but, I do feel it is important to take away the mirror, as the judge. It seems to me, documented health weight standards can provide a better argument than "your thighs are not too big in those pants".

141

Steph seems to welcome the guidelines and the fact that I'm not going to harp at her about everything she ate. She has always been health conscience about her diet. It isn't so much what she eats, but that she does not eat enough of it and uses laxatives to rid her of most of the food she does eat. I don't think it will help her, for me to try to control her intake of food. No.... this is a control she will somehow have to learn to harness on her own.

With Steph back home, we are able to spend a lot more time together, talking about her illness and the worthlessness and the anguish she feels in not being able to control her emotions. Her infamous "shower cries" has helped somewhat but with so many emotions flying around in her mind, it still leaves her with an emotional overload. Listening to her breaks my heart, but it also gives me a new sense of significance to the role I must play in her life. As difficult as it is to hear my daughter express herself in this way, I'm humbled that she feels comfortable enough to share with me her most vulnerable self.

Climbing the stairs with a stack of Phillip's clean clothes, I overhear a muffled ongoing conversation. As I pass the bathroom, I notice the door ajar and the voices are coming from beyond. Continuing on to Phillip's room, I place his clothes on the bed. As I head back towards the stairs, Steph raises her voice with more urgency. Pausing to peek in and see what the commotion is, it all suddenly becomes clear.

"This too shall pass, it could be worse, just keep moving" she says, looking in the mirror with a fierce determination. "It's not as bad as it seems, it really could be worse" she continues, as she takes a few deep breaths. I'm surprised for a moment by this scene, but then it really makes perfect sense. As I back away from the bathroom unnoticed to give her privacy, I can't help but smile at her ingenuity.

As the weeks pass, Steph seems once again to be more stable. She finds a job working as a waitress in a local Mexican restaurant with a friend of hers, believing it will give her a more flexible schedule. Her weight slowly returns to what could be considered normal and she is taking her meds regularly. Though our lives seem to be returning back into a typical family, I fear it's only a pretense of normalcy.

It has now been over three years since our lives were thrown into this nightmarish turmoil and though I have learned much, I'm still struggling beside Steph, to find and maintain that balance that can give her the best chance of a more constant stability. Though we are continually seeking ways for her to self manage her illness; her frail mental state is always at the forefront of my mind.

I find myself struggling daily to curtail the urge to cave into my own emotions over what feels like the loss of my daughter. It's true, only small pieces of her remain and even those small pieces are infrequently seen. As difficult as it is to say, Steph is still a shell of her former self and I miss her sweet affectionate spirit and tenacious mind more now, than ever.

It has been over a year since Steph was enrolled in college and now after months of working at her new job at the restaurant she decides it's time for her to return. While I must admit to being leery, I'm glad a spark of her old determined spirit has returned. It has been a long time since she has seemed up to any substantial challenge and I again force myself to try to be optimistic.

Since the last chaotic episode in the spring her doctor has changed two of her meds again and they are proving to make a big difference in her. Her mind seems clearer than it has in years and we are beginning to see spark's of the old Steph's personality.

For years it has seemed beyond her ability to concern herself with more than her own issues. Now she is handling herself much better, showing the old compassionate concern for others that has been absent for so long. Still, no real hugs are allowed however, slowly but surely, with these new meds

143

my daughter seems to be showing a small resemblance of her former self.

Just before classes start in the fall, Steph tells me she has decided to move in with one of old high school girlfriends, Tina. My memories from the last attempt are still fresh in my mind but, I hold my tongue, partly due to the fact that Tina is fully aware of the dangers of Steph's illness. She is also one of the most responsible young ladies I've ever known and assures me she will keep an eye out for Steph and call me at the first sign of trouble.

The other part, to be honest, is that I'm so very tired and worn emotionally, mentally and even physically from the last few years of this stressful turmoil. I actually find myself welcoming the reprieve.

A part of me feels a tremendous amount of guilt for having those selfish thoughts. Yet, I honestly do believe, I must let her try again for that independence she seems to be ready for and craves, so much. My mind and heart have been in such turmoil these last few years, always obsessing over what the right thing is to do for Steph.

Maybe, living away from home with a friend will help her be less dependent on me while providing the support she still needs. Maybe, I'm partially to blame for her being so dependent. I just don't know what to think anymore.

Steph moves out the beginning of the next month and over the next few months she shocks us all, by doing just fine on her own. She seems to be thriving in her new found independence. As Steph practices the healthy habits that we had determined would help her remain stable, her old determined carefree self continues to manifest itself and hope is again renewed. Surprisingly, I find myself relaxing my grip and begin feeling less a need, to control everything.

We have all heard at one point in our lives, the phrase practice makes perfect. I have come to believe, that phrase rings a profound crucial truth, especially for people with a mental illness. Their precious fragile mind seems to thrive best when they are devoted to a day to day life of repetitive, consistent practiced behavior that fosters stability and calmness they so desperately need. I have witnessed this truth over and over again being demonstrated in Steph.

I've often contemplated this idea of habit forming. We go through our lives doing the same activities over and over again, until it becomes so ingrained in us that we no longer need to think about it. Those practices just become a rhythmic part of our lives and can have positive or, negative results.

What fascinates me is that either way, these influences really just amount to choices we make on a day to day basis. How we choose to tap into those positive influences is ultimately up to each of us.

I have come to believe, these principles need to be encouraged especially in our loved ones with a mental illness. Misfortune comes all too easily for them anyway and without this key ingredient, small things can quickly turn into disaster. It certainly seems to be the case with Steph. It's often painful to watch the destruction play out in the lives our mentally ill loved ones. They need all the help they can get.

CHAPTER 10 Fall 2002

Since I have known Matt, he has always talked about his desire to one day move back to Florida. I have also agreed, from time to time, that when the kids were grown, I would be willing to do so. Of course, this was before Steph was diagnosed with a mental illness, yet over the last few years we have continued to talk about it as a one day possibility. In my heart, I know he was more serious than I have let myself believe and have steadily put him off.

With Phillip, older now and flourishing in his new career, Steph on her own again and doing so well, the reality of such a move, seems more of a looming prospect. I have successfully put Matt off until the children were out of school and grown. Now, all that is holding me back is Steph's illness and of course, having to tell Phillip, he will have to get his own apartment. How can I consider leaving them? When is a parent's job really done? Millions of what ifs, flood my mind as I silently debate the pros and cons of my dilemma.

How can I tell the man I love, the man who has supported and sustained me through the most difficult years of my life with such kindheartedness, no? How can I tell my children, we are even considering this? As I continue to struggle with this dilemma, Matt waits patiently for my answer.

It seems that from the beginning of our relationship; everything has been about me, my children, my needs and my problems. Maybe, it's time to think of him, of his needs, wants and dreams.

147

Underneath the surface of my anxiety about moving, I must admit, a big part of me wants to run to escape all the turbulent drama of the last few years. There is an overwhelming desire sometimes, to hide from my duties as a parent with a child with such a frustrating illness.

I've expended so much energy, trying to maintain the appearance of being strong and just keeping Steph moving, that my nerves feel tattered to the core. At times, it seems like I'm the one who is fragile, not my mentally ill daughter.

A week of fun in the Florida sun, while we visit Matt's Dad, sounds great huh? That is exactly my thought, when Matt proposes the idea to me and I welcome the much needed suggestion, without pause. Well maybe, just a little pause. Since Steph was first diagnosed with Bipolar 1, Matt and I have not taken a vacation, mainly out of my fear that something tragic might happen, in our absence. With a better support system in place, I decide it's time to loosen the apron strings a little.

With our plans all in place, I begin to allow myself the unaccustomed luxury of excitement and anticipation as we prepare for our departure. With Steph's roommate and Dad standing in the wings ready for all conceived emergencies, we pack our bags and race for the airport for what will be our first vacation in three years.

Fall in South Florida, if you've never been, is just about the most perfect weather you can find anywhere. Seeing all the tropical plants in continual bloom, while the rest of the country is getting cold, dreary and turning brown delights me beyond imagination. I have not been so relaxed and at peace in years and with ample prodding from Matt, I begin to see his viewpoint of moving there, in a whole new light.

Admittedly, I'm so overcome with the thought of living in such a beautiful tropical place, I allow myself to be carried away with the prospect, of starting a new chapter in

148

our lives. Thoughtlessly, I push aside the possible consequences of what our moving will mean to my children. Somehow, I even view the idea as a promising constructive force that can help influence them to become, more independent.

And then there's Matt's Dad. Arthur is almost eighty now and definitely in need of someone close by to look out after him. Though still fairly active, it's obvious that it's only a matter of time till he needs some real help. Matt seems anxious to provide that help and I can completely understand. I still feel the pain of loss of my own father, though it's been years since his passing. The one comfort I cling to is that I spent as much time as possible with him before he died. Yes, I'm a firm believer in being there for your loved ones when they need you.

Each time I talk to Steph or Phillip during the week, I discover they are both doing just fine, without me. Though in truth, I'm partly saddened by my not being needed as much as I had believed I would be. I also find myself experiencing an enormous freeing sensation. This only fosters the moving concept, all the more. So as Matt and I leave for the airport, with a lot of coercion from Matt, I agree to make the move to Florida, a reality.

After we arrive back home, I begin to drop hints of how we loved Florida so much. As the scenery in Texas turns into its typical drabness of winter, I'm offered ample avenues to broach this topic. Through out the years, it had not been a big secret around the house that one day in the distant future, Matt and I might move to Florida. But I also thought my children believed it was just a later in life fanciful idea that may never come to pass. We have all joked about Florida being "God's Waiting Room" since a huge number of the American retiree's migrate there for the sunny warm winter weather.

Now that I've made the agreement to move, the reality begins to set in. But then maybe it's just my own

149

reluctance that I'm reading into it. Maybe it's because deep down, a part of me really doesn't want to move away from my family. I find myself constantly worrying about how they will take the news that we are proceeding with our plans, sooner than later.

Being such a worry wart, it's a wonder that I also possess the unwavering belief in personal responsibility, in the conviction that one should be responsible for their own actions, either benefiting or suffering as a result of them. As I sip my coffee on the back porch I begin thinking about this and come to the conclusion that this belief, strangely conflicts with some of my control issues.

Like a lot of parents, I tend to hold myself responsible for my children's problems, struggles and wellbeing, even now that they are becoming adults. I often force my opinions and will into decisions they should be making for themselves. I must be unwilling to let go of that control and the very thought that I am the one preventing my children from growing up suddenly slaps me in the face.

With this in mind, I decide to put into action a new catch phrase, to help me let go and put the responsibility back on my children for their own life issues. And so the phrase, "Oh honey, I'm sure you'll figure it out" is born and put into use. I hope this particular phrase will give them confidence, by showing them I believe they can handle their own problems without me. I also hope this phrase will remind me to turn their choices back over to them.   With anxious anticipation, I wait for every chance to try it out.

I firmly have come to believe that words are much more powerful than we realize. They seem to be a potent tool to help train and encourage our thought process and mindset. They also can cause great pain and frustration, if they are used carelessly.

Once I realized that this was one of Mama's secrets tools, I have tried to use it in my own life help cope with simple daily struggles. This has been reinforced more recently in seeing how this tool has helped Steph regain some control over her own emotions. Most importantly, I have come to believe that carefully chosen words can enable us to stand strong during life's tragedies.

The next Sunday afternoon, the words just suddenly come out of my mouth; "Matt and I are buying a house in Florida and are putting the house up for sale". As soon as the words are out of my mouth I realize that I should have phrased it a little more gently. The silence in the room sends me into a panic. It felt like I was grabbing after a runaway balloon on a windy day. That's the troubling part about words, once out of your mouth, you can't take them back.

Phillip looks at me in shock and says "You're just going to move and leave us here"? As I fumble for an answer, guilt overwhelms me and I can't find the words to make this, better. Matt again, quickly comes to my rescue, "Hey, don't be so worried, we'll just be a phone call away if you need help with money or something." "Beside, it's time you got out on your own; you don't really need your Mom in your way." "You can do this, I know you can…. you're a grown man now."

Though obviously, Phillip is far from being sold on the idea, Steph responds in a completely surprising way by saying, "Oh mom, how exciting". As I press her on how she really feels about it, she simply replies, "Oh Mom, we'll be fine, besides, now that we are grown, it's your time". Looking at me with an unexpected confidence, she continues, "Really Mom, it will be okay!"

True, I will only be a phone call away; available for my famous Mom advice at any moment, even the often unsolicited opinions that I have been trying so desperately to curb. There are also the same banks in Florida, readily assessable to make needed cash deposits into accounts of children in monetary crisis. But how will we cope with those emergencies that invariably will come? Have I become such

151

a main stay in their lives that they will never be able to handling their own predicaments? Time, is sure to tell.

In the weeks that follow, I set aside guilty thoughts and allow myself to become more and more excited about the start of our new life. Reluctantly I turn my notice in at work. Matt seems happier than I have ever seen him. Phillip, though I'm sure is still scared at the prospect of being on his own, gets busy making plans to move out. And Steph surprisingly continues to remain stable and supportive.

The entire moving situation seems to be playing out a lot better than I expected. When we sign a contract on a house in Florida, we stipulate that we not close on the purchase for sixty days. And with plenty of time to spare before the move, we put our house on the market and I begin to sort through years of accumulated stuff in the house preparing to pack.

The weeks are passing quickly and the boxes are pilling up. But life often takes us by surprise. Things can seem to be coasting along just fine and out of the blue, before you can take another breath, the walls just come crashing down. Your heart begins pounding so loud and fast; all other sounds are muffled out. Feeling so completely overwhelmed, the floor seems to just falls out from under you. The force of the crisis seems so great you can't respond, can't even take a breath.

Of all the scenarios that I have feared over the past four years, this is particular situation, I have never really considered. It isn't a crazy wild escapade that gets her into trouble with the law; she isn't curled up in her bed in a psychotic or depressed state, not even an attempt at suicide that I have privately feared for so long.

Preparing dinner one evening I receive a phone call. With a shaky voice, Steph asks, "Mom, are you sitting down?" I know something unbearable has happened, the minute I hear her voice come through the phone. "What's wrong Honey, are you okay?" I reply feeling the growing anxiety. Millions of things quickly run through my mind as some inner instinct pulls me to a chair. "Really Mom, are you sitting down, I need to know if your sitting down?" she stammers.

"Yes, yes, Steph, what is it, what's going on?" I interrupt impatiently. In the seconds that follow, all I hear is a few deep breaths, as Steph gathers her thoughts. "Mom, I....I just took a pregnancy test...twice....it's positive, Mom... I'm....I'm on the pill....I don't know how this happened, I mean I ... I know how but... but it's positive." There is not a word that can describe my feelings; my mind is a blank, void of any coherent thought. My heart is pounding so loudly, for a moment, everything else is drowned out.

It briefly crosses my mind that I'm going to be a grandmother. Isn't this supposed to be a time of rejoicing and excitement? But in reality, all I can think of is Steph. How is she going to be able to handle a baby, when she's just starting to find ways to take care of herself? For most twenty three year old single young ladies and their families, this would be a devastating disappointment fraught with the usual pitfalls of unwed motherhood. But scandal, schedules and financial wellbeing are the least of my worries.

Those normal thoughts never have a chance to enter my mind. I'm consumed with the fears of the possibilities; overwhelming depression, her suicide and even child endangerment. Nausea overwhelms me as I briefly contemplate the possibility of the ultimate betrayal, having to take a baby away from my own daughter to protect it.

Every moment after that phone call seems to be drowning in agony and despair. I don't know what to worry about the most. Nightmares and visions of what this will mean for Steph stay with me day and night. Me.... the go to Mom.....the Mom who has tried to handle anything that has been thus far thrown my way, feels completely helpless.

153

Strangely, Steph seems more together about this than I am. Calmly and quickly she makes an appointment to see her gynecologist for an exam. She asks me to go with her and as we make a list of the questions that are flooding our minds, I can't help but think, she's been on the pill for years, how is this possible?

The thing that seems to concern Steph the most is how her medications might affect the baby. I convince her that since she is already taking her current meds, she should continue taking them until the next week's doctor's appointment. I think the doctor should help her make that determination. I'm too afraid for her to just stop taking them, since I've too often seen the results of what happens when she's off her meds.

As the doctor confirms, my baby is going to have a baby, I crumble inside myself. I've spent a great part of the past few days still hoping that she had somehow screwed up the pregnancy test. When we are told it would be much more dangerous to take her off her meds at this point than to continue taking them, relief floods over me. As Steph completely resigns herself to her pregnancy, she seems to turn all her attention toward taking care of herself and the baby.

Luckily, her doctor doesn't believe the drugs she is currently taking have been shown to cause serious damage to a growing fetus. I'm afraid to ask what would not be considered serious damage, since I know that almost all drugs allege some serious, some not so serious but still unwanted side effects and problems. Though all our questions on the list are answered, I realize the answers only lead to more questions. Now what are we to do? If it could be worse, I just don't see how.

After I drop Steph at her house, I find it easy to allow myself to fall apart. I take full advantage of the freedom over the next few days and again Matt becomes my soft place to fall. I can't eat, sleep or stop thinking about what this

154

devastating turn of events, mean to my daughter. I can't seem to focus any of my energy on thinking of the unborn baby. Not when my own baby's health and wellbeing are in such danger.

What's happening to my strength, my fortitude, and my ability to cope with this difficulty? The only articulate thought in my mind is that Steph can not raise a baby, she's mentally ill! The frustration and resentment over my daughter's illness that I have struggled so desperately to keep buried, that I had thought I had put in a box high on a shelf, comes pouring out. My mentally ill daughter is pregnant and there is nothing that I can do to change that it.

In all the vast quantities of material I have researched on the subject of the Bipolar Disorder; increased sex drive and sexual promiscuity is one of the symptom's that often present itself as a warning of the mania stage. Why has this possible scenario never occurred to me?

Mania has taken hold of Steph many times in the last few years, even extreme mania on a few occasions. Knowing she was on birth control, I must have realized that she was sexually active. Why had I not considered the prospect that she might miss taking this pill along with all her other medications? Why, did I not once, have a conversation with her about safeguarding herself against pregnancy?

Sex and the pitfalls that can come with it, has never been a topic Steph and I discussed very much. Though we spend hours talking openly about everything else, for some reason there is vagueness between us on this subject. It seems to me, sex talks are few and far between in most southern old fashion traditional families. But my embarrassment in broaching this subject seems prudish, if not foolish now.

I'm finding myself spending a lot of time brooding over this failure and am plagued with guilt and remorse for my failure in omitting such an important topic. Why, why, why, why; this small, yet significant word has plagued me for

155

years now? Why did she get mentally ill? Why can't she just take her meds? Why does it take so long to find the right meds? Why can't I accept that I can't fix this? Why haven't I been able to protect her better?

Why, why, why? I can't seem to put them to rest; all the pent up feelings of resentment and anger that I've keep buried inside since the beginning of Steph's illness. And they are now boiling over inside me. I don't know what feelings to give into, the anger, the resentment, the confusion, the frustration, the sadness; each feeling seems to want to take precedence over the other. Nor can I get past the overwhelming feelings of self doubt and always wondering what else I'm overlooking.

A little later in the week I decide that I've put it off long enough; it's time to tell Mama about the baby. Don't get me wrong, it isn't that I'm afraid to tell her that Steph is pregnant. My mother, though a very old fashion traditionalist, is also the most thoughtful and understanding person I've ever known, with an extraordinary perspective on life. I guess it's just that the act of saying those words out loud to Mama will make Steph's pregnancy even more of a reality. And that seems to be something I still don't really want to accept.

As I tell Mama the latest news, she is very quiet at first. Being aware that Steph is Bipolar is completely different than actually hearing some of the bizarre stories I have kept from her.   I'm sure hearing some of the more specific details of what's been going on these past few years, stuns her a bit. I don't know why I have always been so vague about the trials of Steph's illness; she's my mother for God's sake. Who am I actually trying to protect, Mama.....Steph.....or me. Am I even possible embarrassed by my daughter's illness?

After rambling on for what seems like hours, venting and crying my heart out, Mama brings up something that I didn't think of as a possibility. She says, "I can certainly understand how you would be upset, but this baby may be

156

something for Stephanie to focus on besides her illness." As I ponder on these words she continues, "It could be a reason bigger than herself that can make her stronger."

Now she has my full attention. My heart seems to be pounding in my chest, racing to keep up with this revolutionary idea. I attempt to briefly picture it in my mind like a movie, just to see how it could work. Then just as my doubts begin creeping back in, Mama pulls the focus back into view with the clincher. She says, "This baby may very well be Stephanie's saving grace."

Throughout the remainder of our conversation, my mind keeps drifting back to that phrase. It seems like such an unforeseeable phrase of hope. And hope is something I so desperately need, now more than ever. I don't see how it's possible but deep down in my heart I want to believe this baby could be Stephanie's saving grace. And so as the day progresses I find myself wanting to cling to these words more and more with all my heart.

CHAPTER 11 Spring 2003

The next week Steph unexpectedly tells me she is considering putting the baby up for adoption. "I made an appointment with this adoption agency, want to go with me?" she asks with an obvious measure of nervousness. Though I'm not sure why, this question, as it comes out of Steph's mouth, seems to fit my mind as well as a size eight foot in a size six shoe.

I still have not allowed any feeling for this unborn child to develop. It seems I can think only of Steph and what could be best for her. As I agree to go with her, the thought is brought to my mind that she only seems to be able to only think of what's best for her baby. The ever constant protective maternal instinct in both of us is proving to be a powerful force.

The agency is in a large corporate office building, filled with dark mahogany furniture and plush cozy couches. A soft spoken receptionist greets us and shows us to a corner office. The administrator, Margaret, arrives shortly after giving us time to fill out paper work. As she reviews Steph's history with us, a new reality seems to peel back the layers of reality like an onion for both Steph and I.

Margaret seems so nice and compassionate to the circumstances that Steph has found herself in. She discusses the many differing options available which range from completely anonymous to an open adoption where the birth mother even retains visitation rights. Even in explaining the various options, she isn't pushy at all and only seems to want to help all parties involved.

After hearing the answers to all our questions and we leave with a large packet of information and a promise that the agency will not contact us. Margaret stresses that they will leave the ball in Steph's court to play or not. Now the hard part begins and Steph and I spend the next week bouncing the options around.

The next week Steph tells me she chooses not to play, she just knows she could not live with herself making that choice after carrying her baby for nine months. Thinking back over the last week, it should have been clear to me where this was going to go. As the week had progressed, each time we had talked about it she was more and more defensive and negative about the whole idea of adoption.

During the next few weeks, we continue living our lives as best they can. Everyone makes the daily pretense of going to work though I'm not convinced much work is really getting done. I'm surprised that I have not been admitted to a hospital psych ward. I can only surmise that my need to be there for Steph has superseded my need for a nervous breakdown. This entire mess feels so much like a very bad dream.

It reminds me of some of the dreams I use to have as a child. I remember one particular dream where a monster of some kind is chasing me through the woods. I'm running, faster and faster but I keep slipping in the tangled brush. I can't seem to put any distance between us, only staying just steps out of the monsters reach.

As the monster begins to close in, I can feel his hot breath on my neck. My heart is pounding as fast as a freight train in full steam; I can even feel the sweat running down my face. But even as I begin to panic, I find myself thinking, if I could just wake up, this will all go away. Sure enough, just as the monster reaches his claws out to grab me, I wake up.

I'm sure theses types of dreams are probably common in children. Even as an adult I've had dreams where something very frightening is happening to me and I make myself wake up. I find it amazing that our minds kick into a type of survival mode even in our dreams as it tries to protect us in some way. Even in the fogginess of a dream, you can somehow make yourself wake up and stop the madness. I only wish this could work for the current nightmare we seem to be caught up in.

Our lives are filled with choices even though sometimes we claim there is a lack of choices. We sometimes give into panic especially when we feel our choices are narrowed so dramatically by outside forces. Sad but true often our choices are carelessly narrow our own actions or inactions.

I must admit that I often feel myself in a panic from the overwhelming circumstances of the last few years. I feel overwhelmed by what I perceive as the lack of choices even more so now with a baby on the way.

Choices, the right to choose, a woman's right to choose. Who really has the right in this particular circumstance to choose? This has been a debate that has plagued our Nation for years. Whose bodies are we talking about anyway, the woman's or the child's? The topic seems to bring out a deep passion on both sides of the fence.

Coming from a very traditional southern family, I've never thought much about what the right thing to do would be if this situation came about. It's not that an unexpected pregnancy hasn't come up in the circles of my family. It's just that the way it has always been dealt with is to get married and have the baby. As unbelievable as it sounds in this day and age, abortion has never been thought of as an option in my family.

So keeping that influence in mind, you may understand my mindset that the woman's right to choose ended with the conception of life. I have always believed we all have the ability and right to choose to take birth control, to

161

choose to use condoms, even to choose to abstain from sex. But once a child (yes, a child) is in progress our choices are limited to keeping it or adoption.

I have always been puzzled that the debate for abortion never seems to include the protection of the child's choice. For thousands of years, the softer gender has been proclaimed as the protector of life, the amazing single vessel of life itself. What are we as women letting ourselves become? Don't we now seem to be such a selfish gender?

Have we forgotten that we already have a right to choose what to do with our bodies already? We all know that having sex outside of marriage exposes women to the possibility of becoming pregnant among many other health hazards. When will the child that a man and woman often create during this act get a voice in this process?

Oh, that's right; it's not really a viable baby yet, just a fetus. What about the millions of dollars our nation gladly spends on the barley viable two pound babies that are born to crack addicts? Why not put an end to those lives as well? They actually seem to have less of a chance at survival than the near full term babies we allow to be aborted. What about the children of Darfur or Sudan? One could easily argue that they are in just as a precarious set of circumstances as that questionably viable fetus. It seems the slope can get very slippery.

These arguments and the answers to this one issue all seem to contradict each other; for whose benefit, the human who made one poor choice already? The very word viable is suspect to me; just look up the meaning of the word. Viable: feasible – practical – practicable – workable – possible – doable. How many times have these very words been used to stifle women's progress to equality in this country? Yet we as women would deny that progress to a human being even more helpless and vulnerable than we have ever been.

I've often wondered why the same people who support abortion rights so venomously also seem to be the ones who oppose the death penalty. I see this as a complete oxymoronic mind set. How is it that innocent babies deserve less protection than the life of the horrific murderer? Who can explain this to me? Something about this anomaly makes me wonder how the minds of these seemingly compassionate people in other issues can ever think so little of that small piece of humanity that is discarded so thoughtlessly.

I have never really given much thought to how people would struggle with an ideology that has been ingrained in them since childhood. Remember, I am usually a black and white; right is right and wrong is wrong kind of person in pretty much everything. My upbringing and surrounding influences have created a particular mindset in me. Or at least so I thought.

I'm discovering that as people face unusual circumstances the struggle can often sway even the most ingrained of beliefs. And struggle is exactly what happens when the shoe is put on the other foot. And I'm coming to realize how sometimes each of us can squirm when we don't like the fit. This dilemma is an uncomfortable fit to be sure and I find myself refusing to admit even to myself that the squirming of my principles has already begun.

As I discuss this new dilemma with Matt, I find myself trying to justify a change in my beliefs to suit the circumstances my daughter has found herself in. I have always been on the fence just a little, in allowing abortion when it involves the instance of seriously endangering the life of the mother. And I certainly believe Steph's life is in jeopardy at least from a mental health perspective. So, with that little crack in the armor, my hypocrisy takes hold.

After days of struggling within my own turmoil, I approach Steph with the idea of considering an abortion. Sitting quietly watching me try to substantiate my position, I'm sure I must look like someone else's mother, not hers.

The words and beliefs we teach our children often come back to us, hitting us in the face like a freezing glass of water.

Steph and I have had many conversations regarding abortion in general, throughout her teenage years. In those talks, we always both agreed with the belief of the injustice of abortion. As I look into her eyes, I can see that she thinks her mother has metamorphosed into some kind of an alien.

This devastating event in my life firmly gives weight to the principle that exclaims profoundly that a person who has a substantial self interest in the outcome of an issue can be easily swayed. It gives a greater weight to the argument of how a conflict of interest in an issue should be avoided at all cost.

Looking at her, the shame of my wavering begins to pour over me. All she says in response to my request is, "Mom, you have always said things happen for a reason, I was on the pill and still got pregnant. I played my own part in this and should not punish this child for my own mistake." "I will not change what I believe, simply because it's inconvenient to me" And with my very own words simply and kindly returned to me, my request to consider an abortion is denied.

In the days that follow, I find it difficult to even talk to Steph. Riddled with guilt over my duplicity and filled with fear for my daughter's wellbeing, I attempt to pull myself together. When did she become the strong determined one and I, the wavering jelly fish? Is this a sample of what's to come, for her sake, I can only hope so. My lone consolation prize is the pride I feel in raising a daughter who will hold fast to her principles even in the face of such a crisis. That is more than I can say for myself.

These latest events have put on hold my thinking of moving to Florida, but not our actions. Our house continues to be shown by our realtor and in short order we receive and accept an offer. We are moving in forty five days and a big part of me is selfishly looking forward to the escape. I think a part of me hopes our move will persuade Steph to reconsider adoption for her own good as well as her baby's.

Steph is still living with her girlfriend and John, the father of the baby returns into the picture. They quickly begin making plans to live together with his parents and raise the baby together. Steph tells me he is trying to straighten out his life and do the right thing.

Well, I guess that puts an end to my push towards her giving the baby up for adoption. I should take some consolation in the thought that at least she would not be facing this alone. Thankfully Matt continues to reassure me that I am always able to come back to visit at any time at a moments notice.

So in the weeks that follow all of our moves continue as planned. Steph moves in with John. Phillip moves into a small one bedroom apartment just a few miles from the Toyota dealership where he still works. The days pass quickly and it isn't long before we are packed and ready to be on our way to our new home in paradise. Just the thought of Sunny South Florida brings a smile to my mind. A smile that only last until the finality of it all sets in the next Saturday morning as we put the final odds and ends into the moving truck.

Steph and Philip have come to see us off and after many hugs and kisses; Matt finally gets me, the two dogs and a cat into the car. Pulling away from the house, looking in the rear view mirror, seeing both of them standing there on the curb looking like two timid deer's not knowing what to do now, brings tears to my eyes.

As I take the on ramp to the freeway heading east behind Matt in the truck, I begin to sob, heavy gasping sobs. Our cat, Rascal, in her cage on the front passenger seat begins to make drawn out whining meows. With the back seat folded down to give the two dogs as much room as possible, our younger dog Maxi, attempts to pace around in the back seat, stepping on the older Katie. With her calm retriever persona, Katie simply lies there patiently even after Maxi finally calms down enough to sit on her head.

Seeing this comical drama play out before me, my sobs slowly turn to sniffles. In time both the animals and traffic distract me enough to refocus my energies. Then I do as my mother always says; just keep putting one foot in front of the other or in this case one mile in front of the next and place all my faith in our family motto: "this to shall pass."

I can't help but think, isn't our mind an amazing piece of work? How is it possible for me to be sad and happy, fearful and undaunted, confused and determined all at the same time? As the miles roll by, I magically let go of my anxiety for leaving Steph and Phillip behind and let my thoughts be replaced by anticipation for our future. Is the old adage as true as they say, out of sight out of mind? Maybe it is, but more likely, I'm just pushing the guilt to a back corner of my mind to be faced another day.

As we settle into our new home, I continue to talk to Steph and Phillip almost every day. Phillip's phone calls are usually short and to the point, in keeping with his more subdued nature. Steph's calls on the other hand quickly turn into long chatty marathons flooded with her many changing emotions and concerns. Though I still wish I could be there in person to assess her visually, as the weeks pass by, I discover I can easily tell by the sound of her voice and verbal mannerisms, how her day is going.

Days quickly pass into weeks and weeks into months. For the most part she seems depressed, struggling to just keep herself moving. Yet even in her depression she always makes attempts to express determination and optimism. I quickly realize this is her way of trying to convince herself as much as me that things will all work out. Then one day out of the blue, Steph calls to tell me she is breaking up with her boyfriend. I'm not at all surprised to hear that again he is not looking for work which in turn leads to them arguing all the time.

Just from the sound of her voice I suspect that there is more going on but don't want to press the subject, knowing she will tell me in her own time. She had spoken to her Dad the night before and he offered for her to live with them and so she is moving into their two bedroom apartment the next day. I'm glad he is there for her and am also overwhelmed with enormous guilt that I am not.

Should' a, would' a, could' a, that's a saying I have heard often throughout my life. To me, it sums up our regrets for things we feel in our inner being that we should have, could have or would have done differently if only...... Our way of second guessing ourselves and wishing things in our past could magically be redone. Where is that time machine when we need it?

We all have regrets and at times drown ourselves with guilt over some of our past actions. Some things just can't be changed, nor can we turn back the clock on our missteps. But I continue to find myself struggling with the guilt and regret of our move to Florida. With Matt being so happy living in Florida, I just haven't the heart to rain on his parade so I push all these thoughts and feelings deep down inside myself to face another day.

I quickly find myself consumed with talking to Steph every day, often two and three times a day. I have an overwhelming need to hear her voice, to let her just talk and hopefully be some sort of support and comfort to her. While I believe Steph has a real need to talk, I also must admit my own need to be of some help is growing most likely from the bottled up feelings that I have abandoned her.

Often times I hear from Phillip who is called upon by Steph to rescue her from her growing car troubles. You know dead batteries, flat tires and even a belt or two that breaks. He always makes time to help her when she calls and frequently calls her to remind her of needed oil changes, brake checks and to put on slightly used tires and rims he is allowed to accumulate for her at the dealership where he still works.

On days when I feel the most panicked about Steph, I call Phillip to suggest he meet with her for lunch just so he can give me feed back on how he feels she is doing. His report is always his typical short and to the point; "She looks fine but she's just so scatter brained." He often expresses his concern for her car and doubts over how long he can keep it patched together.

After hearing of Phillip having to rescue her and her car in the middle of his work day for the second or third time, I comment to him about how much things have changed between them. We laugh at the memories of their childhood and teenage years and how Steph had been the perfect Big Sister, always looking out for Little Brother. Then I say to him with the utmost sincerity "you do realize that you're the Big Brother now."

He just makes his usual slight chuckle and says with an abundance of pride in his voice," Mom, I've been Big Brother for quite a while now." Wonders never cease; who would have thought the tables would have turned so sharply.

Soon after moving out of John's house and into her Dads apartment, Steph finds that is unable to wait tables at the restaurant and being so far along with her pregnancy, weeks pass before a friend helps her obtain part time employment at a day care. As with other times of unemployment, we have to help with her bills. Even though living with her father, she still has to pay for car insurance, her storage unit, medical co-pays and most importantly to me, cell phone bills. This financial burden is the least of my worries and helping her in this way partially appeases my growing guilt for us moving away.

Several times during these months I call Steph's father to get his perspective of how he feels she is doing.

Though he tries to assure me she seems fine, he also mentions in each conversation how much time she spends in bed. I empathize with his concern since I am more than familiar with what that means. I too have witnessed the effects of her depression so often and having my fears confirmed only magnifies my guilt and feelings of helplessness.

As her last trimester of pregnancy arrives, Steph tells me she has gained lot of weight, more than her doctor is comfortable with. He encourages her to keep her weight gain to a minimum if any at all during the final stages. She begins retaining water, her feet swell and her blood pressure begins to climb. This concern only adds to her stress and depression, which in turn increases the triggering of more migraines. Hearing about all these things only reinforces the premise in my mind how much a person's mental health is connected to good physical health.

As the big day draws near, I can hear the tension rise in Steph's voice. Nervous over what is to become of her and the soon to arrive baby, she seems to be consumed with making headway in her mental stability so she can care for her baby. Often during our phone calls she makes the comment that's not just about me anymore. In her determination to overcome her depression, she suddenly becomes obsessed with taking the best possible care of herself.

Though a little surprised about the change in focus, I'm glad to discover that she is making such an effort to do many of the things I have been trying to encourage these last few years. Eating healthy, sleeping regular hours and trying to get more exercise, most importantly taking her meds religiously have all suddenly became a top priority in her mind. I'm so thrilled that she is finally taking these things all so seriously. I eagerly hold my breath in the hopes that her new mindset will be a beneficial and lasting new regiment.

With only two and half weeks remaining until her due date, Steph's doctor puts her on bed rest. Due to his

169

concern of over her high blood pressure and the swelling of her feet and hands, fears of toxemia merely add to our list of misgivings. And surprisingly this time the least of our worries is that Steph is out of work once again. Pregnancies are always filled with worries, apprehensions and nervousness as the big day draws near; but I can't help but think, what more can Steph, in her already fragile mental state, endure.

With my reservations to fly home the day before Steph is due in place all that is left for me to do, is to wait and hope my timing's in sync. But as they say, timing is everything and sometimes all of our best laid plans are made for naught. Steph's doctor suddenly decides to induce labor a week early and disappointment sets in as I realize, I'm to miss the birth entirely. I had no idea I would be as excited and anxious as I am, fielding calls from Steph and her father as to how the delivery is progressing.

As the day passes into evening, Steph's condition turns more serious as her blood pressure continues to sharply rise and fall as she nears the time for delivery. As the next hour and a half goes by, I pace around waiting for the news, hoping things are going well. Knowing it should be any moment, the lack of information is tearing me apart. This seems to be taking way to long, why isn't someone calling me? I know they must be busy but did they all forget that I'm here, fifteen hundred miles away, desperately needing to know WHAT'S GOING ON!!!?

Almost another hour goes by before the phone rings. My heart swells a lump in my throat as I'm told there was a problem during the delivery. There was some meconium in the amniotic fluid. I'm told that this means the baby passed its first bowel movement in utero (as he passed into the birth canal); it's a sign of fetal distress. In addition he managed to inhale the meconium with its first breath getting the substance in his lungs.

With Steph's blood pressure yo-yoing like it has been, I'm not surprised there was fetal distress. I'm told that Steph is fine for the moment but the baby is not breathing on his own and he has been rushed to ICU. Apparently when this sort of thing happens it can cause very serious respiratory complications. Did I hear the word HE? I almost forgot, I had been told the baby was to be a boy! A little boy in trouble, as I hang up the phone my heart breaks.

A few minutes later Steph calls me in tears. The pediatrician has just told her that her baby is not breathing on his own and may not live through the night. If he did make it, he will most likely have brain damage. Since they are at a small branch hospital that doesn't have a neonatal trauma center, he is going to care flight him to their main hospital in Dallas where he can get better care. Just hearing the devastation in her voice I feel so helpless.

I ask how she is doing and she tells me they are having trouble getting her blood pressure under control but that they are going to release her so she can drive to the hospital to be with her baby. This makes no sense to me; shouldn't they transfer her with the baby? I should be there in command, telling those doctors what they should be doing! Who releases a new mother from the hospital just three hours after a troubled delivery when she is still having blood pressure problems?

I tell her I will be on the first plane out to Texas in the morning. As I hang up the phone, the shock of it all overcomes me. I can't believe this is happening with me almost fifteen hundred miles away. With my own mind in such a fog, Matt thankfully takes over and calls to change my flight, hotel and rental car reservations.

As he helps me pack, Steph calls again to tell me John, the baby's father, is taking her to the main hospital. She will call me as soon as they get there and find out what's going on. I remark that I'm a bit surprised that he has shown

171

up for the delivery. Then Steph quickly tells me he has shown interest lately in being a part of the child's life.

After many calls throughout the night confirming no change in the baby condition, no sleep, tears overflowing, I get on a plane early the next morning bound for home. What could have prepared any of us for this? Life is often sprinkled with tragedy, in our case I feel as if it's been more like a flood during these last few years. Frustrated and a bit panicked I can't help but think that this plane is just not going fast enough.

Landing, taxiing, riding the bus to the rental car center, waiting in line, these are all necessary things that seem to be taking forever. DFW Airport is almost an hour's drive away from the hospital but living in the Dallas area most of my life, I know my way around. I find myself being thankful that North Dallas early afternoon traffic is surprisingly light. I talk to Steph twice during my drive trying my best to remain calm and be reassuring as I listen carefully to try and judge how she is holding up.

I'm a little puzzled, each time I ask her how her blood pressure is doing, all she says is, "I'm fine, I have to be". She seems to be so focused on her baby; she refuses to worry about her own health. With her mental health being my number one concern, I ask her about her meds. Seemingly almost annoyed with the question, Steph quickly replies, "Yes Mom, I sent Dad to get them last night, I'm taking them religiously." "I can't afford to have another episode ever again."

Of course I'm worried about the baby, but my main concern at the moment is for Steph. As I approach the hospital, I phone Steph again to find out what parking area I should park in. Knowing that I will see her in moments, she tells me that this morning, while I was on my flight; she had to be taken down stairs to the emergency room. "What? Why didn't you tell me this?" I asked.

"I just didn't want you worrying about me while you were driving" She replies. It seems that her blood pressure rose too high and they had to give her medication to help lower it. Steph went on to tell me that the nurse had questioned her about why she had not been transferred with the baby for her own continued care. Since she wasn't their patient, they said all they could do is give her some medication and require her to use a wheel chair to keep her off her feet until she goes to see her gynecologist.

Hanging up the phone, I wonder to myself, if they were really all that concerned about it, why they didn't just admit her. As I enter the hospital I can't help but think that none of this is making any sense to me. My baby is on blood pressure medicine and in a wheel chair less than twenty four hours after having a problematic emergency birth? Something is horribly wrong with this picture.

As I enter the waiting room, I scarcely recognize her sitting in her wheel chair in the corner. I knew Steph had gained a lot of weight during the last months of her pregnancy but she is so puffy and swollen. This person doesn't look like Steph at all. It seems like yesterday that I was so concerned with her extreme weight loss. The once tiny frail young lady now looks to be at least eighty pounds heavier.

As she turns to look at me, I see an enormous amount of pain in her eyes, pain yes, but also a focused clearness in her eyes that tells me she is stable and holding her own. I don't know how, but she is showing a strength that I have to admit even I couldn't pull off. As I take a deep breathe somehow, I gain enormous strength from this vision of the strong young lady before me.

For months now, since the moment Steph told me she was pregnant, I have purposely not allowed any feelings to develop for this baby. I feel like I have too much to worry about already and have refused to think about what it would be like to be a grandmother. In fact, I never have understood

173

all those grandparents who are constantly shoving pictures of their precious prides of joy in everyone's face while telling the countless stories of their grandchild's unparalleled genius. Yeah, yeah, yeah, they're all cute, aren't they?

As Steph gives me a quick update on the baby's condition, I feel a strange sense of relief that he is now off the respirator and breathing on his own. Since all the neurological tests are not back yet, she doesn't know yet what kind of problems he will be having. I marvel as I hear Steph say, "I'm just so glad you didn't have to see him with all the tubes and monitors hooked up to him." It seems funny to me that not only does she not look like My Stephanie; but there is also a determination in her voice I have not heard in years.

Moments later with Steph beside me, we enter the Neonatal Intensive Care Unit or as we will soon become accustom to calling it "The NIC U". As we approach the second door, Steph leads me to a steel sink. She instructs me to thoroughly scrub every millimeter of my skin below the elbow. Minutes later I'm being strapped into a sterile gown and lead through a half glass door. As my eyes adjust to the dim light, I scan the large room.

I feel very much out of my element as I pass several unbelievably tiny babies that are hooked up to a wide variety of tubes & monitors. Such fragile babies as these would have lived only seconds if at all only a few short decades ago. A powerful unseen force slaps me in the face, just from the sheer reality of seeing what modern technology can do for these tiny beings. Astonishment doesn't begin to describe the weight of this force.

As we approach the back corner of the room, Steph quietly greets a small young lady in pale scrubs. Steph easily brushes 'off the nurse's questions about her own health, instead proceeds to introduce me to her. Anxiously she asks the nurse for an update on the test results for her child. "Nothing yet, Honey, just be patient, he's hanging in there considering what he's been through" the nurse softly replies.

174

As we step past the nurses station Steph turns to me and with such pride and tenderness says, "Here's your grandson, Dylan Michael, do you want to hold him?" I have never been a big believer in love at first sight. Nope, not me, I'm not a fan, I just don't buy it, I don't see how it's possible. Loving someone means knowing them, their character and qualities, who they are as a person, doesn't it? But as Steph moves to the side, I look down and fall completely and hopelessly in love. How is this possible?

There are defining moments in each of our lives, some that we can classify as truly life changing experiences. As I reach into the crib, gingerly lift him into my arms and look upon his sweet face, my vision begins to blur. I realize in this precious moment, my life will never again be the same. As I blink away the tears and look over at Steph, I also know in my heart that somehow she has magically been transformed into a Momma Bear.

CHAPTER 12 Summer 2003

The next four days are a frenzy of rushing back and forth between the NIC U and Steph's doctor's office. Suddenly the doctor seems to be very concerned about her blood pressure fluctuations. I can't help but think, a little late for him to be so worried don't you think? Each day as Steph's blood pressure rises and falls adjustments on the new medication has to be made. We rush to the emergency room twice because her pressure goes too high or suddenly drops too low.

This lack of control, I'm sure, is at least partially due to the stress she's under. I'm finding it a difficult task getting Steph to stay off her feet as ordered, much less getting the proper rest she needs. In her new role, her main concern seems to be only for her newborn son. I constantly seem to be reminding her that she must take care of herself because of Dylan. I soon find myself frustrated in my own change in role as grandmother.

However with that being said, I also feel an enormous amount of pride and affinity towards the emerging Momma Bear. Even though Steph is stressed and exhausted, she seems to also be totally focused and in charge of her own mind and emotions. With only a few instances of breaking down in tears, she is showing remarkable strength and determination in spite of this tragedy. I must admit she's holding up extraordinarily better than I ever expected.

Each time I enter the NICU, I find myself astonished by the difference in the size of my grandson in comparison to the other babies with special needs. Dylan's weight at birth was just over eight pounds. In contrast, not one of the other fragile babies is over four pounds, most being considerably under even that size. He just doesn't seem to belong in here; he looks to be the epitome of a perfectly normal newborn. Looks apparently can be deceiving, for I'm fully aware that with the huge cost involved, they wouldn't have him in the NIC U unless it was absolutely necessary.

Each time a report or test comes back from the lab, we are given cautiously better news. At his birth, we were told he may not live through the night, and then he did, albeit with serious respiratory problems. Next, we are told he will but most likely have severe brain damage, yet each neurological test returned so far shows within normal parameters. It seems Dylan is beating all odds and as far as his mental abilities, we will just have to wait and see how he develops and progresses in the years to come.

Though he was quickly removed from the respirator just hours after arriving at the NIC U, he still remains on oxygen. Several times a day he is given various medications through breathing treatments. His respiratory system, damaged during birth, continues to present fears of pneumonia and in addition to him now being labeled as chronically asthmatic.

We are told that this not so little boy will need careful and conscientious long term care. Pausing to contemplate all these uncertainties only renews my fears in how these added responsibilities will intrude on Steph's own abilities to manage her own illness. I quickly become mentally and emotionally exhausted just considering these separate yet soundly connected problems and the many possible ramifications.

True, Steph seems to be more than holding up mentally and emotionally. I'm impressed but baffled with her resolve and determination to stay strong and focused on Dylan's health. I seem to be constantly switching back and forth between concerns for her and her baby. I continually have to tell myself to keep putting on foot in front of the other, just keep moving, in hopes that, this to shall pass.

As we each face our own personal trials, we all struggle to be strong, be brave and above all to keep hope alive during these times. I have tried to be more adapting at this process especially since Steph became ill. Looking back, I'm glad that these sentiments were always discussed and stressed to both of my children during their upbringing. I've come to realize that Mama's secrets have been a crucial key in all our struggles.

As a young child, Steph had shown great ability to apply these sentiments, that is, up until the time she became ill. Since those days, the effort has been sporadic and with obvious amounts of exertion. It has been many years since I've seen this type of determination and I begin to allow myself to see hope and give credence to the theory Mama spoke of not so long ago. This child may very well be Steph's saving grace.

Each time I'm permitted to hold Dylan, I feel a strong irreversible bond rapidly forming between us. He seems so perfect to me in every way and he is becoming more and more priceless in my heart with each touch. I must admit that I feel great shame in these moments as I also remember my discussion with Steph all those months ago, when I wavered in my conviction against abortion. Now, I can't imagine the thought of his life being considered as so unimportant.

The saying," time heals all wounds" applies perfectly to many of life's circumstances and situations, but all I can hear in my head is a newly created saying reverberating in my mind, "time wounds all heels" for that is how I have come to view myself; as a vacillating heel.

As I spend time during the week with Steph and boyfriend, John, I find myself being encouraged by his new mindset. In awe of his new son, he seems to be committed to

179

trying to be a good father. Though a part of me is skeptical that he has the ability to make such changes overnight, John promises to do what ever he needs to do, to insure his place in their lives. I allow myself to be somewhat convinced by his sincerity. I mean, people can change, can't they?

Steph is persuaded to give him another chance and quickly they decide that she will move back in with him before Dylan comes home from the hospital. I understand her desire for John to be involved, Dylan will need a father. I just don't see the big hurry; I'd rather wait and see the sincerity of his commitment in the next few weeks. Only time will tell, if the promises he has made can endure this test.

Due to all the medication's Steph is on, she always knew she wouldn't be able to breast fed Dylan. This fact presents an extra disappointment now especially with the current medical belief that doing so can give great benefit to children with his type of problems. Nevertheless, he is devouring and digesting his formula with abandon. Dylan's respiratory condition seems to be improving each day and thus far, all neurological response tests imposed on him seem to be completely contrary to the original medical professional's belief.

By the end of the next week Steph's blood pressure stabilizes somewhat and plans are in place for her to move back in with John. The NIC U doctor's begin to talk about the possibility of a release date for Dylan in the near future and it seems the critical stage of this trial has passed. Though things seem to be looking up, I continue to wallow in my customary and what I perceive to be justified worry and guilt. As the time comes for me to return home, anguish and sadness crushes me with its heavy weight over what I will be leaving behind.

As I leave for the airport I am bombarded with encouraging reassurances from Steph, Mike, John and even Phillip, each trying in their own way to set my troubled mind at ease. Little do any of them know, inside my mind or my heart, I can never allow my inner turmoil to be at rest. I see it not only as a virtual impossibility but, as my duty as a mother and grandmother to worry and fret and over what is, most certainly, a just cause.

In the days and weeks that follow, Dylan is released from the hospital, Steph's blood pressure ever so slowly returns to normal and the day to day grind of caring for an asthmatic and allergic infant takes shape. Steph quickly becomes adapt at giving Dylan his numerous daily breathing treatments and medication. The dreaded chore of removing the never ceasing streams of mucus from his nose is another matter all together. This unpleasant chore, done with a modern day barbaric device, no mother ever looks forward to.

Promises, promises; they are sometimes broken even under the best of intentions and sometimes are made to begin with out of a need simply just to appease the circumstances at the time. I sense frustration mounting between Steph and John over his lack of looking for a job, his temper and from also what I suspect to be his continued or resumed drug use.

I'm sure, out of her sense of loyalty to him; she only makes vague responses to my questions on how things are going with him. However, at this point in our own relationship, I'm more than able to read between the lines.

It isn't long before the affirming call comes. With a shaky voice, Steph tells me, "Mom, I just can't continue living with John any longer." "I asked Dad last night if we can move back in with him," she continues. Frustration in her voice is clear as she explains that Mike is renting a truck and moving her back into his apartment that very day.

I have the feeling I'm not being told the full story. I strongly sense that much more has happened, but with Steph and the baby secure in Mike's care, I resist being too inquisitive. She obviously doesn't want to tell me everything. So letting sleeping dogs lie and instead focus all my efforts on calming and encouraging her.

181

Steph, trying to make the best of a bad situation, just keeps saying "I'm okay Mom, it could be worse". I get the distinct impression she's trying to convince herself as much as trying to set my mind at ease. In her younger years, she had always been one to put a positive outlook on situations and now, even in the face of her illness, she struggles to make an extraordinary effort to keep an upbeat attitude.

The phrase "things could be worse" is another one of Mama's gifts to us as we were growing up. It embodies an outlook that she has tried to engrain into all of us since our childhood. This is one of the creeds Mama lives by in an effort to help us learn how to endure through hardships and to keep all things in perspective. I believe most of all, this lesson is to keep us from sitting on our own pity pots over our personal tragedies. Still to this day, Mama always makes the extra effort to look on the bright side of everything.

Every one of us, as we struggle in our own lives, can easily look at our own situation, whether it be an illness, financial crisis, or even a death, what ever it may be, and find someone else just as easy with a much more tragic or difficult set of circumstances. Just think of any difficult situation in your life, then think some more, I suspect it really could be worse.

To help make my point, just imagine a couple with a child who has a terminal illness. While this is horrible in it self to imagine, it could be worse. That couple, at the same time, could also be going through an irreparable divorce or one of the parents could suddenly be killed in a car accident. As I said, it could be worse.

Now what if, during this same crisis, that lone parent also lost their job? Then top it off with the thought that the small apartment they lived in is destroyed by fire. And while we are imagining, let's put them in a third world country. You see, it always, always could be worse.

If we can keep this in our mind through our struggles, it can serve as a very valuable tool. It can help to keep us from falling prey to those debilitating thoughts of self pity and desperation. Thoughts that stifle us and prevent us from seeing or even hoping that there is a light at the end of the tunnel. Those feelings can paralyze us into unfocused inactivity. This inactivity alone can prevent us from climbing out of our current crisis and just wallow in a hopeless pit of despair.

I often contemplate on all of these precious truths that Mama stresses to me and I have in turn tried to pass them on to my own children. I have found them to be a source of inspiration, hope and encouragement to us in those difficult times. As I take a step back and ponder over Steph and her life I truly believe these phrases and the forging of this type of mindset just might be the catalyst that helps sustain her in her mental health struggle.

These thoughts bring to the forefront of my mind, a need I believe is important for parents to understand and practice these types of encouraging words and outlooks. It seems to me that impressing our children with such positive thoughts can be as crucial to their wellbeing as anything else we do for them. I think it's important to encourage, in any way we can, the spirit of determination, resolve and hopefulness in our children from infancy to adulthood and beyond. There is no magic crystal ball that can allow us to see what will lie ahead of them. But I do believe it's important to keep in mind that they will need every tool imaginable to face the unimaginable.

So, with these thoughts fresh in mind, I persist and struggle to stay focused on the task I have assigned myself, listening, supporting, encouraging and monitoring from Steph from afar as best I can. Being a mother it seems is a task that never ends; it just evolves anew with each changing phase of the relationship. This particular task I'm afraid, is far beyond my own means or abilities.

183

As the weeks turn into months, seldom does a day go by that I do not speak to Steph at least once, more often than not, two or three times in a day. Our closeness seems to be growing into something far beyond the normal mother and daughter relationship. True, we have always been extraordinarily close, but it has now risen to an entirely different level of dependency, a need that desperately cries out to be filled on both sides of the phone.

I feel an immense sense of urgency in her need to have someone she can spill her heart and emotions out to and I'm more than willing to try and fill that role. It has become the greatest purpose in my life and everything in my world stops when she calls. I readily listen to her ramblings for as long as she needs.

Even though Steph is often frustrated and depressed, feeling worthless and disheveled, by the end of each of our conversations she usually seems more in control of her emotions. I'm beginning to believe that she really just needs to express the turmoil that is screaming so profoundly in her mind, once that's done, she can take a deep breath and continue on with her life.

Being a mother seems to be giving Steph a great sense of purpose and she is determined to be the best mother she can be in spite of her circumstances. During each phone call, I can almost hear it in her voice; a resolve to get the reassurance and support she needs, to give her strength to keep pushing forward. It seems this child of mine will always amaze me.

In spite of all the turmoil that she has been through, I am thankful that Steph's immediate everyday essentials are being met. She has a place to live, a small bedroom she shares with Dylan. She still has a car, not quite what you would call a sweet ride but it still runs, for the moment. Dylan is on Medicaid and she is still on Mike's medical insurance. Though most days she still struggles to keep from curling into a ball, the fact that she is so determined in the fight to hold her own can't help but make me proud.

In spite of her minds tendency to be dragged into despair, Steph's focus and care of her son is proving to be exemplary. She is exactly the type of mother I thought she would be all those years before she became ill. It seems to me that her deep love for children and most precisely her own child is relentlessly driving her to stay focused. Apparently, even her mental illness can not hold the Momma Bear in captivity.

Regardless of how she is feeling, she seems to be forcing all her energy into her son and the significance of taking the best possible care of her own health takes on a whole new meaning. Steph tells me of a routine she tried a few years ago, one she uses when she is feeling herself slip ever so slightly out of control. "I just go into the bathroom and talk myself out of it" she reveals. As she describes it, I can vividly remember seeing her standing in front of the mirror all the years ago. With tears in her eyes frantically repeating the phrases over and over again, "just keep putting one foot in front of the other", "it could be worse", and our family favorite "this too shall pass". Again I'm reminded of the power of these words and the effects they can have on a mind in crisis.

With her still on Mike's medical insurance, Steph doesn't have to worry about her own health care cost since everything is covered except for the co-pays. Shortly after Dylan's birth she changes her anti-psychotic medication again and only time will tell if there are improvements in regards in her mental health. So far, so good, at least this one is not making her sick or sending her into an overwhelming stupor like some of the others have in the past.

Since Steph had so much trouble with her blood pressure during her delivery and was not at all happy with the way her gynecologist released her so quickly after delivery, she requests to see another doctor in their office for her follow ups. It is apparent to me that she has lost confidence in him and frankly, so have I. So when the time comes for Steph's six weeks check up, I'm all ears the morning of her appointment waiting to see what she thinks of her new doctor.

When the phone rings, I feel a great sense of relief by the excitement in her voice. Steph tells me, "I really like her, Mom." She continues by telling me that they decided to forgo birth control pills. Since she was on them when she got pregnant, they both decide to take more drastic steps in prevention.

So, with that in mind, Steph opts for a type of an IUD device that remains in place for up to five years. This new assurance gives her great peace of mind knowing she will not be surprised by another pregnancy. I'm a little taken aback by the relief I feel in hearing this news. I didn't realize I was even concerned about the possibility of another pregnancy.

Also since Steph insist that she always took her birth control daily, her gynecologist takes the time to research medication interactions. She easily discovers that the medication, Zyprexa, Steph had been taking before she got pregnant has shown in recent studies to virtually nullify the effects of the birth control pill. I'm astonished that something as simple as an unwanted drug interaction has changed our lives forever.

It seems to me that someone, her regular pharmacist, her original gynecologist, or her psychiatrist....someone would have known and alerted her to this possibility. Didn't they all have a list of all the medications she was on, even the birth control? Are they all just uninformed or did they just not think it's an important piece of information to a young lady? For days I allow these questions to plague me.

This new piece of information begins to open up an entirely new avenue of awareness for us both. It seems that what we don't know about how the medications we take and how they work together or against each other are a crucial aspect of our well being. After searching the internet for days, I've come to believe that anyone taking a medication should discover everything about how it works and what can alter the performance of that medication.

For instance, I discover in my search that when taking some anti depressants, the positive effects and benefit of that drug can be diminish or even nullified just by drinking grapefruit juice. I also learn that when you take certain types of anti depressants you shouldn't even take certain over the counter cold medications. Sometimes, mixing these medications can even have tragic results.

Discussing this very topic with my neighbor, my findings were only reaffirmed as she told me about a young lady that she knows that is also Bipolar. It seems that this young lady, we'll just call Suzy, has been on anti depressants and anti psychotics for several years. Recently after catching a cold, Suzy purchases an over the counter cold medicine from her local drug store. Not realizing the conflict in combining these particular medications, she takes it just before going to bed that night.

Late the next afternoon, Suzy's roommate finds her dead in her bed. An autopsy report soon shows that Suzy tragically died from the combination of her prescription medications and the over the counter medication. As I think on this story for a minute, I realize this is a normal thing most of us do all the time when we catch a bug. But as shown in this heartbreaking example, can prove to be very deadly.

So it seems to me that each of us must be hyper diligent in understanding every single thing we take. There seems to be a very good reason for telling your doctor everything we take, including even over the counter products. This must be why it's important to use the same drug store for filling prescriptions or purchasing any of these other remedies.

Pharmacists, I have discovered can provide a wealth of information and protection and we should probably use them as our lives depend on them, because it seems in some circumstances it most certainly does. I find it tragic that this key piece of helpful information is a key that most people probably wouldn't consider when making what seems to be very normal purchases.

As Steph becomes more empowered with the additional tools of not having to worry about more accidental pregnancies and a clear awareness of the dangers of conflicting medications to safeguard her health, it seems to reinforce the idea that she, above all others, need to be responsible for her own wellbeing. As I ponder this new mind set, I begin foster the hope that this could be another one of those most important influences in Steph's struggle to maintain her stability.

As our lives continue on, so do the never ending phone calls that constantly seem to weigh heavy on my mind and heart. Though it's emotionally exhausting for me to listen, encourage and support her every day, I don't feel I have a choice really, this is my role, my duty as her mother. In some ways I think it's the least I can do after moving so far away.

Some of these calls are filled with tedious nonsensical babble and tears from her frustrated feelings of worthlessness. But, often she is just calling to tell me about Dylan and how he's doing. Bragging as most mothers do, about the amazing things he is learning and how he continues to surpass all childhood development charts.

Then again often it's just conversations that are simply about what her plans are for the day. In any case they all seem to revolve around her need to have someone to talk things over with, the good as well as the bad.

Living with her father, though cramped, at least relieves her from the stress of providing a roof over their heads. However, she still needs money to support herself in other ways. Car insurance, gas, storage, cell phone, diapers, formula, doctor co-pays as well as co-pays to fill her prescriptions, all these things still have to be paid. Many things we all take for granted cost money, money she doesn't have. As all single mothers' do, she needs to find another job.

Forget that she is now far behind on her credit cards and has never paid off her student loan she received during the last attempt at the community college. Forget that she is now also being sued for damages from the car accident she had a while back and even more, forget that she still owes on a car that was totaled during the last accident. Forget that she still owes on a broken apartment lease. Even finding a job will not solve those issues. No, those issues will just have to be placed in a box, put on a shelf for another day.

All things considered though, Dylan is progressing very well both physically and mentally. Steph is so dedicated to his breathing treatments and other aspects of care in regards to his asthma and allergies that he seems to be having few significant problems. Her patience with him is never ending; now everything seems to be about "The Baby" and I mean everything, even taking care of her own health.

Each time they see the pediatrician, Dylan is proving the initial evaluation of having some sort of brain damage as being just flat out wrong. Every test and assessment shows him to be completely normal. Nevertheless, the doctor continues to insist he be tested and evaluated every step of the way until he starts school, just to monitor his progress. Steph is thrilled with each confirmation that Dylan is beating the odds and proving those horrible predictions to be in error. I can't help but think, yea, finally, some good news.

With our worries over brain damage dramatically lessened, Dylan's asthma and allergies continue to be the main concern. Steph seems to be more and more obsessed with doing his breathing treatment exactly as prescribed. Additionally she focuses on keeping him away from smoke, pets, dust and anything else that seems to set off his allergies and asthma. Her performance is paying off, with only a couple of minor asthma attacks so far, though his allergies always seem to be aggravated by something.

After months of watching me worry over her, Matt decides it is time for Steph and the Dylan to come for a visit. I'm so excited I can scarcely contain myself. Watching me, field daily calls, fret continually over her stability and be an emotional basket case these last few months, I guess is more than he can bear. Being a man with a need to do something to help, his offer could not have come at a more perfect time. Steph has found another job and is set to start work in two weeks.

Standing in Terminal 3 of Fort Lauderdale Airport, I can't wait for the plane to land. It has been almost four months since seeing them and my heart is ecstatic beyond the imagination. As I wait, it seems like for hours, for them to come down the corridor towards me, my anxiety is almost overwhelming. I know the plane has landed, where are they?

As I spot Steph slowly making her way toward the security exit, struggling with her new baby, his diaper bag, a carry on bag and her purse, my eyes well up. To me, in a way this vision epitomizes the aloneness of her struggle in her life. There is a certain amount of determination prevalent on her face even in this small example. It seems there is always just a little too much to handle but she is so stubborn, she just won't give up. This image makes me smile, even through my own motherly pangs.

Reaching out to her just as my tears begin to flow, I suddenly find myself clinging to her with our precious bundle of joy sandwiched between us. Although, I feel her stiffen, giving in to that need she has to protect her personal space, I appreciate that at least she doesn't pull away this time. A measure of sadness comes over me as I realize how much I still miss the real Stephanie.

190

During the next few days, watching Steph in action as she cares for her son becomes an amazing experience for me. Each task is performed with such immense patience and determination. She seems intent on doing everything possible to insure that her son's allergies and asthma remain under control. Seeing them so up close and personal brings to my mind the brilliantness of the maternal instinct.

Though her mental and emotional state I still consider to be fragile, it's obvious she is of the mind set that she must prevail. This is not someone who is ready or willing to give in to defeat and wallow in her feelings of hopelessness and despair. I can see something in her changing dramatically, or maybe I should say, returning.

In all our lives', there come a time when we must say something to a loved one that may seem to be hurtful or even cruel, but the importance of it, is so profound that the subject must be broached. As difficult as this particular discussion will be, seeing her determination and devotion gives me the needed confidence that the time has come make a crucial and possibly unwelcome promise.

I know Steph is fully aware that my most consuming purpose in the last few years has been to protect and help safeguard her out of my concern for her mental illness. Even during her pregnancy and delivery, the utmost priority in my mind has always been for her welfare. However, now, I recognize in addition to my daughter's wellbeing, I must also consider the protection of my new grandson.

I have no idea how to begin such a delicate subject as the one plaguing my mind. The last thing I want to do is hurt Steph or send her into an emotional or mental tizzy. All things considered, there's no turning back now, I have to proceed. I have learned my lesson; never again will my being uncomfortable with a topic, be an excuse to fail in what I now feel is my duty.

The last afternoon of their visit, with Dylan sleeping on my bed, Steph and I can't seem to pull ourselves away. As we sit next to him just admiring his adorableness, I ask, "How are you really holding up, you know, mentally.....emotionally." Feeling a little uncomfortable, knowing where I intend to go with this conversation, I hurry along "It's just that you have a lot on your plate and I've been worried about you."

"Oh, there are days" she says, "when I don't think I can handle it." Looking down, smoothing Dylan's blanket with her fingers, taking a deep breath she continues. "Days when I feel like I'm going to fall apart, but then looking at him, I know I have to."

Quietly she admits, "And that somehow makes it easier, easier for me to take the best possible care of myself." She looks down at her son again, smiles and says "I have to be stable, so I take my meds religiously and just keep moving, you know, there is no other choice; none of this is about me anymore."

With these thoughts hanging in the balance between us, I decide to take the next step to make my case. I know in my mind the moment is right. As gently as possible, I tell her, "I think I should tell you, honey that if the day ever comes that you are unstable, you know, to the point that I feel you can't safely care for Dylan, I hope you will understand and agree that I should step in." Nervously, I quickly add, "And maybe even take him from you, you know, until you are stable again."

As my mind races with fear and my heart swells an enormous lump in my throat, I wait for her response. Time stands still between us, as tears well up in her eyes. Somehow even though I believe we are so close, I find it odd that I have no idea what she will say to this assertion. As my nervousness grows, I notice Steph taking another deep breath.

"I expect you too, Mom," she says, "thanks, promise me, you will". Her answer, it seems to me, reveals the old sound, always reasonable and determined Steph I knew all those years ago. Relief washes over both of us as we hug and burst into tears from the strain over the importance of this topic.

Later that night as I lie in bed pondering over our conversation, I'm wrapped in a blanket of delight in this transformation. A mere six months before Steph had not been able to achieve anything more significant than getting her self out of bed. Now, she is not only finding the ability to push her self into caring for her own mental health, she's also proving to be an excellent mother. As I peacefully drift off to sleep, I wonder what else is in store for my amazing daughter.

Though Steph's time with us, four days, is considerably shorter than I would have wanted, it's such a relief to see her, to judge visually for my self how she is doing. As I see them off at the airport, I realize the great assurance I have gained in knowing that I do have the ability to somewhat judge her stability from long distance. These thoughts give my heart and mind a measure of peace. However, in spite of that peace, I still find myself crying all the way home.

CHAPTER 13 Fall 2003

During the few days before starting her new job, Steph shops for some new clothes with some of money we gave her on her visit. Still considerably overweight from her pregnancy, none of her old work appropriate outfits fit her yet. Most of her wardrobe still consist of old hand me down maternity clothes and buying new clothes gives her a boost in confidence.

Before coming to visit Steph had researched and checked the references of several day cares in her neighborhood, trying to find one that is economical yet demonstrates the best concern for taking good care of her asthmatic son. Again we pitch in to pay for the enrollment fee and the first two weeks of services. Steph is excited and nervous as she starts to work the following week.

During the second week of her employment, Dylan catches his first cold. During the night he has an asthma attack and has to be taken to the emergency room. Doctors stabilize and release him to go home by morning. Steph however, misses the next two days of work due to a respiratory infection and high fever.

Steph spends those days doing everything possible to keep his asthma under control; breathing treatments, and using a humidifier, plenty of liquids and of course the dreaded nose sucking device that all babies show such distaste for. After returning to work, Steph quickly realizes that she is also coming down with the cold. Suffering through as best she can while working, she worries she will give the cold back to her son. Thankfully that doesn't happen and for the next few weeks life goes on.

Life goes on that is, for three more weeks until again, Dylan gets sick. Three more days of missed work and doctor's visits pass before she is able to return. It seems another problem rising to the forefront is that Steph has no back up day care and Dylan can't be dropped off if he has fever. What choice does she have? It worries her to drop him off anyway since each time he has a respiratory or ear infection, if he isn't cared for properly the risk for an asthma attack increases substantially.

During the next few weeks, I impatiently wait each day till Steph gets off work so I can call her. Consumed with hearing her voice and knowing she and the baby made it through another day with out mishap, all I can do is pray. I'm sure some days, my calls are annoying her to no end, but worry constantly runs heavy in my heart. I feel a small measure of comfort in knowing she is not completely alone, since she is still living with Mike.

Steph still has concerns about John's drug use and I'm relieved to discover that she is not allowing him to see his son very often. She told him when she moved out that until he straightens up his life, he will have minimal involvement with Dylan. So with the John's lack of participation, so goes his family and any help they might otherwise provide.

With Mike and his wife both working and Matt and I living in Florida, the lack of grandparents available that are able to fill in as back up daycare, only compounds her problem. Who do young parents turn to nowadays, with everyone working or living so far apart from their loved ones?

It seems guilt will forever be my prominent emotion. I can't seem to stop thinking, oh, how I wish things were different. Then just as I begin to feel really down about everything, Mama's voice magically whispers in my head "look on the bright side, remember, it could be worse." So, I force myself to take a deep breath and smile.

Looking on the bright side is a little easier when I consider that the medication Steph is currently taking seems to be keeping her mentally stable more than any other past combinations. The regimen now includes a high dose of Effexor, along with an anticonvulsant and migraine treatment, Topamax that has recently been shown to be effective in treating those with rapid cycling Bipolar mood swings. Most recently added to the mix, 10 milligrams of Adderall which she began taking shortly after Dylan was born, to help her focus and concentrate.

As I think back over the last few years, I find myself amazed at how the use of some of these various drugs are now being used as valuable treatments for mental illnesses. It's fascinating to me how the medical profession is finding uses for them other that that which they were originally designed for.

Thankfully, we have fearless scientist and medical professionals who are discovering more and more, how these chemicals can have different affects on the mind. I'm encouraged by the current research and headway they are making in understanding the workings of our mind and its needs.

Of course one of the problems with trying all these different drugs is the side effects. Steph's most frequent complaint about all the meds she had tried was that they put her into such a dopey stupor. Then in turn, she felt her depression would take hold more firmly.

Other times she felt some kept her from thinking clearly or as she often described it, "feeling so scattered I can't put two thoughts together." Several of them made her sick at her stomach; some made her dizzy and have tingling feelings in her hands. A few of them made her heart race so fast that she went to the hospital thinking she was having a heart attack.

Of course, with Steph doing so well now, it helps that she finds it imperative that she consistently take her medication so religiously. Even after seeing these new results, I have to concede, even if only to my self, that the past medications may have done more for her if, she had always been so consistent in taking them. It's crossed my mind lately that some of her complaints could have just as easily been caused by withdrawal symptoms when she would abruptly go off her meds.

As our nightly talks continue they seem to be filled with a renewed sense of openness, an openness that seems to help to fill both of our needs. Mine, to hear a stable, calm sounding tone in her voice and hers, to have someone to just talk everything over with, concerns and feelings that are continually racing through her fragile mind.

My mind is put at ease somewhat since, I believe, I can judge her mental state, just by hearing her voice. I can't seem to stop myself from always asking her if she is taking her meds, eating and sleeping regular. I just hope I'm hearing the truth. It seems, not being in control will always be a delicate issue for me. Finding ways to support her without feeling like I should be taking over apparently is a chore still beyond my current ability.

Days often come and go when she seems so much more subdued and I worry that depression is trying to take hold of her. Consumed with feelings of hopelessness and worthlessness, Step is frequently concerned over her lack of financial ability to live on her own. Though she is still working, each time I hear this subject, my frustration grows from the inability to have a solution ready at hand for her. It seems all I can do is listen to her and try to be reassuring that things will get better and remind her that "things could be worse".

On the other hand, there are plenty of days when her excessive chattiness generates fears in my mind that the dreaded mania feature is preparing to pounce. It's all too familiar to me what can happen next. It usually starts with becoming extremely restless, staying up all night unable to get proper sleep. If not brought under control it could lead to wild shopping sprees that play havoc on her check book. Left unchecked, her thought process could easily get so distracted and disoriented, she becomes delusional. Not a pretty picture and these possibilities don't even encompass the worse case scenarios, which I no longer allow my self to imagine.

Just days before her three month review, Steph calls me in tears. "Mom," she says through her sobs, "they told me my services are no longer required". No explanation is really needed, due to Dylan's illnesses; she has missed too many days of work. We weren't really all that surprised; employers do need reliable employees. And so, after crying and taking two days to regroup, the job hunt resumes for Steph, once again.

As Steph pushes on, so do I, in an effort to do what I can to keep her focused and stable from afar. My efforts to encourage her often seem feeble and meaningless to me. Thankfully Matt remains my source of strength and support. Always showing so much understanding regardless of the unlimited amount of time I devote to her.

It seems our lives are continually interrupted by my concern for Steph. But no matter what drama interrupts what we are doing, his patience never wears thin. Always encouraging me to keep it up, reminding me she wouldn't be calling me so often, if she didn't find a measure of comfort in our talks. Most importantly, he was always allows me to fall apart then, somehow patiently consoles me and helps to pull me back together.

During the week that follows, Steph calls. "Mom, I just got another job" she declares excitedly. But concerns over leaving Dylan in day dare are playing havoc on her mind. How long will it be before he has yet another ear infection, cold and/or asthma attack? While these are worries any working mother has, if you are Bipolar everything becomes magnified and yet keeping your stress level as low as possible is an imperative component in maintaining your own stability.

Nervously fidgeting with a hangnail on my thumb, a habit that Matt has all too well learned to read, my mind is swimming. "I know she is under enormous stress" I confess as we sit on the back porch. "I'm worried that it will send her over the edge, you know, she's just too fragile" I continue, just as blood turns the underneath of my nail red.

Thinking back through the recent conversations with her, I know that, though her reasoning and determination seems sound, I can hear the nervousness and anxiety in her voice. Matt reminds me, "You have to hang tough through this; she needs you to be strong." With firmness in his voice he adds, "You know you can't fail her now." As usual, my take charge kind of guy pushes me to keep the hope alive that "this too shall pass".

As the weeks pass, the daily phone calls continue usually as she drives home from work. Any time she calls me during the day I panic, in fear that Dylan is sick again. Relief floods over me each time I hear that that is not the case. Often it's just a call to get a pep talk on her lunch break. Sometimes, even better, just to tell me about some great feat my grandson has accomplished.

Other than his illnesses, it seems that my daughter is blessed with an easy baby. Rarely does Dylan cry and whine as other babies often do. He seems to save his fussing for only when his nose or chest is congested from his allergies or a cold. His demeanor for the most part is happy and content even through an ear infection he had during his last cold. This easy going temperament often reminds me of another easy baby I adored more than twenty two years ago.

With all that being said, there have been several occasion's during these recent weeks when she calls me frantic, saying that the day care has called and she is on her way to pick Dylan up early due to a fever. Also there has been several times, when she calls mid morning to tell me she didn't go to work because he is running a fever. Doctor's visits frequently report ear infections and/ or another respiratory infection causing more missed work. My heart begins to grow heavy with fears of another impending termination that I know must come.

Towards the end of Steph's third month of employment she is let go again due to excessive absences. While neither of us is really surprised, this continued frustration sends us both into a deep pit of anguish. Steph fully understands her employer's position in needing people that can make it through the first ninety days without missing work, but she is at a loss as to what she can do about it, her son's health must come first.

As the next few months rolled by, Steph frantically searches for another job and she keeps Dylan part time in day care to give her enough free time to go on interviews. Revising her resume, struggling to put a positive spin on having such a wide variety of jobs is proving to become more and more difficult. Finally after three long months she is offered another office position and our lives return to the old familiar ritual of daily phone calls sprinkled with anxiety.

Well, I could just as accurately say the old familiar ritual of anxiety. As it often happens, things in our past inevitably will come back to haunt us. One day, not long after Steph's March birthday, she goes to renew her driver's license and is shocked to learn that it has been suspended. What? When? How? Why? These are the same questions Steph ask as she stands trembling in front of the clerk at the Department of Motor Vehicle in shock.

The root of this story goes back to when she had that car accident a while ago; yes the same one she had during the

201

insurance lapse. It seems the other party and their insurance company went to court and received a large judgment against her. Part of the judgment included the suspension of her driver's license for failure to provide insurance.

Since she had moved in with her father, they didn't have her new address therefore; she did not get her notification. Apparently, Steph has been driving with a suspended license for months, unaware.

The plot thickens, according to an attorney, in order for her to get her license back she will have to either pay the hefty judgment or file for bankruptcy. Will this madness ever end? It seems for the last few years, each step forward leads to two steps backward, sometimes three.

So, following the attorney's advice she files for bankruptcy and then applies to get her license back. Weeks pass before she is driving legally and pushes on with her life. True to her ever returning determined nature, the energizer bunny strikes again.

It doesn't make Steph feel any better knowing and accepting that most of the problems she faces are self induced, at least in some way. If she had taken her meds she might not have let her insurance lapse. This in turn led to her insurance company not paying the claim and not having her car replaced. Then of course, this led to her losing her job and therefore her apartment. This is a blatant example of how small individual things can often have a snowball of effects.

Continually, I find myself struggling with the mindset of how much personal responsibility does Steph really hold for these events. After all, she has a very detrimental mental illness. I, in an attempt to make her feel better, find myself often saying things like," well honey, you have a serious mental illness, and it's not all your fault". Steph, with that practical mindset of hers, just as often replies "Mom, the lamp is still broken."

This phrase is a simple analogy I often used in her childhood in an effort to teach personal responsibility. I always wanted to stress to my children that, you may realize and accept you did something wrong, you may in fact be very sorry for it, but "the lamp is still broken" When harm is done, a price of some kind must still be paid. That was the way it was taught in the world I grew up in. Sometimes I think this is an important value that is missing in a lot of young people today. Excuses are too easily made and too easily accepted.

As all babies do, Dylan grows quickly during the first year. He is plagued by his allergies and asthma constantly, even with Steph's obsessive care of him. These problems are often aggravated as a result of a cold catch at the day care. Steph soon discovers the day care is not giving the breathing treatments to him as needed. She has suspected it for a while and after a little more careful observation and monitoring of the daily amounts that should have been missing yet are not, quickly proves her correct.

Steph is furious, realizing this lack of care is a big reason he keeps having so many problems. Without the treatments, his asthma goes haywire making his allergies flare up, resulting in a runny nose that increases fluid in his ears, and then inevitably turning into an ear infection. The other often scenario is his allergies increase, congestion filling his chest leading to a bronchial infection; neither outcome can be very pleasant for him.

His pediatrician ultimately recommends putting tubes in his ears to help drain the backed up fluid. Convinced this could make a difference for her son's health, along with a change in daycare, the surgery is scheduled. Time will only tell if these two changes would help resolve some of his problems and give relief to her absentee's.

The day before my grandson turns one year old, Steph losses her third job, again due to past absences, but this time with a new twist. Early in the morning, the apartment building just across the parking lot from theirs ruptures in a blaze, fire trucks seem to pour in from everywhere.

The entire complex quickly becomes blocked in and the main street in front of her building is closed. She can't get her car out to go to work, no one in her complex can get out, but that doesn't matter. Already having missed so many days when she calls in to work to tell them, it seems to be the final straw that breaks the camels back.

Though each loss brings about added stress and anxiety to Steph, Matt and I often remark that Steph resilience is astounding. Each time, with amazing determination she somehow bounces back and pushes herself forward. No matter what life seems to throw at her, she just keeps going, just keeps fighting.

It reminds me of the old watch commercials seen frequently during my youth, demonstrating the resilience of their product. The phrase "takes a licking and keeps on ticking" caused an explosion in the sale of these watches back in the seventies. Matt and I soon begin to refer to Steph as our little "Timex", watching in amazement as she bravely takes on everything that's thrown at her. Hindsight though, is always 20/20; and as we look back, though now we can see plainly how she fought each step of the way to overcome each of her trials, those days of living in those crazy moments gave us little time for reflection.

I must admit however, each time she looses a job I can't help but wonder, are her absences only due to her son's illness? Steph's history of losing jobs was present long before her son was born. I find myself continually in my own mental argument during each absence, and as follows with most things I feel regarding Steph, the guilt soon follows for doubting her. It seems somewhere along the way, I've lost my knack for objectivity.

In my heart I want to believe she is doing everything she can to keep herself healthy while struggling with her son's reoccurring respiratory problems. Yet, those memories of her not so very distant past seem to be keeping me from completely trusting. Too often, I'm reminded of those disruptions her mental illness has brought into our lives. As with anyone, those behaviors create suspicions and doubts that are not easily put to rest and I struggle with this dilemma often.

I've discovered that this is a common dilemma among families when one of its members suffers from a mental illness, especially so, with Bipolar disorder. Years of watching and supporting them through the turbulent ups and downs and repeatedly finding out that their loved one has again stopped taking their meds, lead to enormous frustration and mistrust. It seems those of us who supposedly have a sound mind, can often find our own minds confused and in turmoil as a result.

As I talked with Phillip one day, I discovered I'm not alone in my dilemma. Though he says he is always ready to help her with her car troubles or anything else he's called upon to help her with, he admits to me that he has often found himself frustrated with his inability to understand what's going on with her. But recently he has found that choosing to "not" try and understand her and just help when she needs him has helped him to put those thoughts to rest.

As I vent my own frustrations to him over her inability to keep a job, he sensibly tells me I'm just going to have to accept that Steph is doing the best she can. I had never thought of my son as being wise and perceptive, because of his lack of academic abilities I always seem to view him as a bit of a simpleton. But as I step back from the situation, I realize his mind set is probably not only the healthiest and the most mature but also extremely astute and insightful.

Since the beginning of Steph's diagnosis, I have had the most difficult time understanding and accepting this new reality. In a way I must admit, it somewhat annoys me that

205

Phillip would be the one to have discovered so easily the best way to handle the feelings that come from that lack of understanding.

It seems those of us who do not struggle with a mental illness can not, nor will we ever be able to, fully understand what goes on in the mind of a person that suffers with one. I guess to me, not understanding is and always will be the hardest part and it only makes accepting more difficult.

Only days after my conversation with Phillip, Matt, knowing me like a book, prods me for what's on my mind now. Of course he knows more than likely it has something to do with Steph. As I dive into a tirade about my inner turmoil and conflict, Matt pours me a cup of coffee and points toward the back porch. After only a few minutes, he interrupts me and suggests that since I believe so much in the power of words; why not try another use of words? Impressed with his own ingenuity, with a smirk he quickly begins reciting his own mother's favorite prayer.

"God grant me the serenity to accept the things I cannot change; courage to change the things I can; and wisdom to know the difference."

Just hearing the Serenity Prayer seems to bring a twinge of peace to my mind. So committing myself to this new mantra, I push myself forward wanting to believe and trust that Steph really is doing the best she can. Letting go has never been a strong suite that I could lay claim to. But for my own sake as well as Steph, I know I have to establish and put into action these words before I drive both of us over the edge with my nagging and conflicting emotions.

As I put into place this new prayer, I find it allows me to zero in on the impression I have of just simply being amazed by Steph. Amazed by her determination and resolve to somehow find a way to beat the odds of being a successful parent with a serious mental illness. Amazed, that she refuses to give up in the face of job loss after job loss, refuses to even give in completely to those feeling of hopelessness. Amazed, that she refuses to give into the feelings of worthlessness and despair that seem to plague her daily. Amazed, that she even refuses to give into her own self imposed failures.

Most people in her shoes might find it easy to blame everything on being Bipolar, but not Steph. It seems she is not going to use the insanity plea as an excuse. She fully accepts that she was the one who had not paid her bills causing her insurance to lapse, and she was the one who had not protected herself from pregnancy. She was the one who had gone off her meds over and over again. The more I think about it, the more I realize that Steph sees being Bipolar as only the avenue that her tragedies travel on.

During these same months, Steph and I have many conversations regarding some of the criminal cases that are in courts around the country. These murder cases involve people that are obviously suffering from some form of mental illnesses and these defendants are almost all asking for leniency or acquittals because of their illness.

Steph expresses strong views on this subject and rejects the idea of using insanity as a defense for their heinous crimes. In her mind, yes, she can certainly understand how their illness has lead to their actions but doesn't believe that their illness should excuse them from the consequences of their horrific actions.

After all, the victims are still dead and even though they might be unable to control themselves mentally, they should still be held responsible for their actions as well as held in check against future detrimental actions. Explaining her thoughts with passionate conviction Steph says, "Always giving in to the excuses, only allows a person to escape the fight all together." "And I think being in the fight is a big part of what keeps a person pushing forward."

Thinking on this for a minute, I ask, "Is this why you never seem to want to give yourself even the smallest break?"

What was her simple response? "Mom, I know that if I give myself an inch, it can be such a short distance to taking a mile." Though the Momma Bear in me still wants to give her some slack, I also find that my admiration for her apparently knows no end.

And so with these thoughts in my mind as the weeks pass, with remarkable determination, I watch her continue to fight, every step of the way. And with each step, I watch her proudly and my amazement can only grow for "Our Little Timex". I begin to allow myself to see a glimmer of hope and search for the root of her inspiration. As time passes I begin to give way to the idea that maybe, just maybe, once again my mother could be right. As Mama had continued to say "This baby may very well be her saving grace."

CHAPTER 14   Summer 2004

He has large hazel eyes, light brown hair and a smile that can't help but light up the room. With his first birthday come and gone, he has developed into such an easy going, sweet natured, clever as well as comical little boy. Rarely does he fuss or cry, even in the midst of his suffering from the illnesses that continue to plague him. He's remarkably like Steph when she was a small child, with an added touch of comic relief, which I find to be reminiscent of his Uncle Phillip.

As all grandmothers would be, I find I'm captivated with him and all his adorable little behaviors. Just the way he puts himself to sleep is precious, just place him in his crib and in goes his thumb with one hand, and then he fervently begins twirling a top strand of his own hair with the other. And yes, I'm aware all grandparents believe their precious grandchild is perfect. But that's okay; I will do my best to be extremely good for his self esteem and this is one role I will most assuredly enjoy playing.

While he is still bothered by his asthma and allergies, the tubes placed in his ears seem to be doing their part in draining the excess fluid, keeping ear infections in check. Getting the breathing treatments so religiously has proven to help keep asthma attacks at the minimum. And the new family owned day care where he now attends consists of grandmother type teacher's that are more than happy to take an active role in all aspects of his care.

While these improvements help to cut down on absences at work caused by my grandson's illnesses, Steph is still under enormous strain. Oh, she puts on a brave face and does her best to keep moving in her new job, but her mental and emotional state is still very fragile. She always seems to be just on the verge of falling apart. Yes, she fighting it every step of the way, but the exhausting effort she has to put forth is taking its toll.

Just after my grandson's first birthday, I go home for a short visit. I'm thrilled to see both of my children and new grandson. Though Steph seems to be doing well, concern over her weight resurfaces the minute I see her. She is very thin and pale and I quickly mention how much weight she has lost. She says that she is eating well and simply places the blame on her medication, Adderall and explains that the drug is known to cause drastic weight loss.

While I already knew weight loss is one of the side effects of this drug, it still brings up fears that her bulimia has returned. Trying not to be too obvious, (ha, ha,) I begin monitoring everything she eats and watch her for frequent trips to the bathroom. As the week goes by I begin to realize that everything else seems to be in order, her hair is shinny and thick. She has what I would call a healthy appetite, she even seems to relish in having ice cream and other fattening treats.

So reluctantly I try my best to push the fears aside and trust in her. We have several very frank talks about her weight during the week. And one day as she tries to put my mind at ease, she mentions that her best friend from high school who had recently helped her secure her new job is also concerned about her weight loss. Just knowing this particular young lady is again a part of her life gives me a measure of peace. After being out of touch for years, it seems their friendship has picked up right where it left off, as close as ever.

As I spend time with my grandson during the week, I quickly rediscover what an exhausting chore it is just chasing after a toddler. Keeping up with his medications, breathing treatments, keeping his nose cleaned out and nap times, I feel a little out of my element. These experiences only reaffirm to me that practice makes perfect and when that practice is absent the perfection can dissipate dramatically.

I find it amazing that Steph is handling all these chores plus trying to work a full time job in the midst of a mental illness. It's no wonder she is so emotionally and mentally fragile at times. I like to think that I'm of a sound mind and as I try putting myself completely in her shoes, doing all she is attempting to do, I'm not sure how sound I would be, even with my so called sound mind.

The last day of my visit Steph confides to me that she is still having a difficult time concentrating on the tasks she is required to perform at work. Though her absences have been reduced somewhat, she admits she is often late for work or has to go home early due to a migraine. As she tells of the numerous times she has had car trouble and had to call Phillip to rescue her thus making her late, I find myself winching. Again, I have to push the doubts out of my mind; concerns of what this means and my suspicions of the regularity of her taking her medication.

Even though I proclaim my amazement at her determination, I am also forced to revisit the possibility that my daughter may never be completely self sufficient. Her mental illness may never allow it and living with that thought, is becoming more and more difficult to ponder. I can only imagine what thoughts like these, are doing to Steph. How does one continue to push them selves forward, when they are faced with doubts such as these, faced with job loss after job loss?

The one thought that often gives me some comfort is that if not for her determination and perseverance, traits which were so strongly ingrained in her throughout her childhood, she might be in a completely difference place even now. I have come to believe that those who do not put these traits into daily practice often find themselves in and out of psych wards or even worse….in the grave.

It seems persistence, fortitude and resolve are imperative to the triumph over most of life's obstacles. This belief is what I must cling to in hopes that Steph can overcome the difficulties of living with a mental illness. In spite of all these doubt, I can't help but appreciate the fact that things could be, should be and actually have been worse, much worse.

Phillip on the other hand, still working at the same Toyota dealership has become an impressive mechanic, continually absorbed in learning everything he puts his mind to about automotive mechanics. Who would have thought that the young teen with virtually no skills or ambition would have turned into such a steady work horse? The more money he makes the more he wants to learn and the snowball only grows as time goes by. It seems there is not enough grease in all of Texas to squelch his fascination with cars or drive to earn a living.

I have learned through this particular experience the importance of not giving in to the misgivings and negativity a parent may face when it comes to a child's abilities. I see now that focusing efforts on helping them finding their gifts and encouraging them is a much more productive avenue. I only wish I would have recognized it years ago and saved us both all the stress and uncertainty of his teen years. Just seeing my son so happy as well as successful in this line of work makes me so proud of him and his unexpected accomplishments.

No, he's not a millionaire, not even close, but he is thriving, paying his own bills and Lord knows, this country will always need honest, dependable, knowledgeable people to repair their cars. Who knows, one day he may open his own shop, even start a chain of shops. I, for one, will never doubt his abilities or ingenuity ever again. No, it seems my role is and always should have been one of a positive encourager and cheerleader.

Steph on the other hand is always a puzzle to me and what my role really should be. I find the task of just encouraging and cheering her to be a constant struggle. I always seem to want to do more for her, not believing she can do it on her own. And since I am not mentally ill, I don't think I can fully understand the wide range of difficulties she faces or what her needs even are.

It seems that none of us will ever really know how much of their mind they do have control over even with medication and structured positive and practiced behaviors. I just know in my heart, it is a struggle I must somehow overcome; I must keep in mind Phillip's words, "She doing the best she can". God grant me the serenity.

The next week back at home, the daily phone calls continue and are filled with her constant need for reassurance and my feeble attempts to calm the shakiness I hear in her voice. It a ritual that has long been established as we try to sort through the various emotions that continually flood her mind. My daughter, her illness and the concerns that come with it are always on my mind.

More than ever, I feel like a life line to her stability and though exhausted from my own efforts and worry, I believe I must persist in my self imposed duty of being the sounding board for her many conflicting feelings. At times I think that maybe a part of me just needs to believe this presumption so I feel like I'm actually accomplishing something.

Even though each trip home causes me such pain, seeing her, still remembering her as she was all those years ago; just being there, judging for myself that she's still in the fight gives me a measure of peace. I must admit that small piece of reassurance, gives me strength to believe that she is doing the best she can. It seems that again I must recognize

213

that my greatest struggle is still putting aside the loss of who she was and accepting who she is today.

I still find myself grieving for the old Steph so much, just in the simple things like her easy joking manner or her insightful compassion. I can't remember the last time I saw one of her brilliant smiles that use to bring such delight into a room. I think most of all, I miss her warm affectionate nature; she just seems so stiff now. What I would give for just one of her hugs.

As the next year passes, Matt proves to stand by his commitment to send me home at least twice a year as well as supporting me in my inner turmoil. I often wonder where he gets the strength to remain my rock. Where do any of us get the strength for that matter? The older I get, the more I have come to believe, it is not something you're born with; but something you just have to make your self practice, even when you don't think you have it in you. Maybe it's like the old Nike commercials has always proclaimed; just do it!

It seems others in Steph's life are making great strides in their life. Somewhere during this year, my grandson's father made some life changing decisions. I don't know if it's due to Steph limiting his visits with his son or if he finally just decided to grow up, but he has given up his drinking and drugs, even quit smoking cigarettes and has found a good job installing alarm systems.

Though Steph is somewhat leery of his ability to have a long term turn around, she has begun to lighten the restrictions she had placed on him. As the months pass by he is proving to be not only to be a tenacious worker but is also making great strides in becoming a more active father. Since being an active father is so new to him, he makes mistakes and errors in judgment from time to time. But in this case too, we are trying to keep in mind that practice can only improve.

Looking back on his situation, I can see a similarity to Phillip in the sense that he did not have an academic personality. He seemed to have an extremely low self esteem and due to these two things he always seemed to be caught up in the use of drugs out of his frustration. As he found a job that he could learn and be a success in, he has quickly begun to blossom. The encouragement is causing snowball effects of improvements in him in all aspects and for my grandson's sake; we couldn't be more pleased.

After seeing this effect manifested several times now with in my immediate circle, I have come to appreciate the positive influence of a persons self esteem and how even small incremental steps moving forward can greatly it can change a person's life. How a person feels about themselves seems to be a catalyst to achievement, even a precursor to success.

Again it brings to the forefront of my mind, the importance of encouraging our youth even those who are lacking academic acumen to seek out their individual talents and abilities. What kind of country would this be if everyone was a doctor or a lawyer? What kind of people really keeps this country running?

It truly does take all kinds and we should not only encourage it but appreciate the variety. I for one am thankful, to have a well running car and an alarm system. I am thankful that my trash is picked up, and that someone can repair my roof for me. Without different people meeting our different needs, we would have a very serious problem. Whatever one's talent is, it is important that they pursue it, and their friends and family encourage it.

We all have young people in our lives that are not what we might consider to be bright; they struggle through out school, often even failing remedial classes. It seems that these are the minds we with need to encourage their spirit of determination the most. Yes, learning to read, write and perform basic math skills is crucial but also finding an avenue for our youth to earn a living is paramount.

I know a few ways to foster this spirit, is to let them help repair things around the house if they have an aptitude for this. They could be taken to Home Depot or Lowe's, where they actually have free "How To" classes for young people. Enroll them in auto mechanic's or shop classes at school. If they are artistically inclined, sign them up for classes at the YMCA or YWCA, even local craft stores have various types of classes for young people or even let them paint their own room. Helping them search for their talent and interest and then giving them some practical experience can do wonders for the encouragement of their self esteem. Not to mention that if they actually see some of their accomplishments it will most likely spur on that spirit of determination that we all so desperately will need in life.

I've learned how crucial it is to help them find reasons to be proud of their abilities, something I know I should have learned years ago. It seems that sometimes I focused so much on Phillip's lack of academic abilities that it only pushed him further into frustration and discouragement which more than likely lead him to feeling hopeless. I know, I failed Phillip for years in this regard and am thankful Matt saw through all the muck and turned him towards auto mechanics. As a parent I can see how I failed in my responsibility to help him discover other avenues of success.

This thought only reinforces my mindset to continue to encourage Steph in her own struggles. As she continues to live in the small apartment with her father, Steph loses two more jobs, wrecks another car and yet somehow manages to keep putting one foot in front of the other.

Each circumstance brings about another bout of depression, yet each time somehow she pulls herself up out of her despair. Determined not to fail, to be the best mom possible, not to be a helpless mental case, my Little Timex kept on ticking.

I struggle with my own mental frustration and emotional exhaustion as I attempt to fulfill my role from afar.

216

Anxiety, guilt and anger continually conflict with my feelings of pride and amazement towards my daughter and her fight with her mental illness. I often wonder how other mother's with mentally ill children deal with this very personal traumatic set of circumstances. Surely, I'm not the only one who is facing what feels like the loss of their child.

I turn to the library in search of books written by parents in this position looking for a sense of commonality. Yes, I have Matt, Phillip, Mama and others in my life who know Steph, who are connected emotionally to her and share in my heartache, but none of them are her mother. I alone, am her mother, and I can't help but feel isolated within my turmoil. I have an overwhelming need to feel that someone is walking this road with me, literally knows what it's like to walk in my shoes.

What is it that makes us want to seek out camaraderie to share in our similar endeavors? Just knowing someone else has been through the same circumstance can often give us enormous strength to continue the fight. Finding strength in numbers has been a mainstay used by all civilizations throughout history. This strength can lend us the courage we need to face yet another day, to step by step simply walk one more mile.

Yet even as I ponder on this topic, I have to wonder, what gives my daughter her strength and courage. It's amazing to me, that Steph hasn't given up; I can't keep count anymore of how many jobs she has lost, how many car accidents she has had, how many checks she's bounced all due to her unstable mind. If the saying is true, "what doesn't break you will only make you stronger" she must have the strength of ten thousand women.

Surely in spite of her strength she must feel desperately alone, yet she doesn't seem to want a support group, to have a need to be surrounded by other's who struggle with this mental illness. Steph just says, "I have my psychiatrist and you to talk to, what more could I need?" She doesn't want her life to be all absorbed in the mindset of being "Bipolar'. She so desperately wants to just be normal again.

Maybe a part of her is much healthier than I am. Maybe, I'm wallowing in self pity over what I still see as the loss of my daughter. A large part of me feels shame in the fact that I still don't accept that this is my daughter. This is who she is now, when will I adjust to the new reality?

It seems I've spent these few last years of my life overly absorbed with the phone. I always seem to be waiting for the phone to ring, talking or should I say listening to Steph on the phone, or being emotionally drained from being on the phone. If I don't get that call, I find myself stressing about why it's not ringing and spend sometimes, hours trying to reach Steph on the phone.

My frustration only rises with each new situation that comes along and I struggle with overwhelming feelings of restraint with my inability to find any real solutions. Nothing I try seems ever seems to work, at least not for long. I always seem to be right back where I started, frustrated and in a panic. I can't imagine what Steph must be feeling as she struggles with her constant unpleasant companion.

Suddenly, a notion comes to my mind like an old movie. I picture myself out in the ocean, just enjoying the feel of the water and sun on my skin. Farther out than I usually go, suddenly I find myself being pulled out into the ocean. As I swim harder and harder in an effort to reach a shoreline that is smaller with each passing moment, thoughts of far away deserted islands pop into my head. Will I survive the inevitable shark attack that will surely come long before I arrive? Panic sets in and I frantically try to remember what the experts have advised.

Those of us who live or frequent the beaches know what every lifeguard and the national weather service constantly tell swimmers who find themselves caught in a rip current in the ocean—to survive the danger of these currents that can pull even Olympic swimmers out to sea must be handled in a very specific way. We must remain calm, think clearly and do not; I repeat do not fight against the current. Once you get a grip on yourself, you are told to swim parallel to the shoreline until you no longer feel the pull of the rip current. With the pull of the current gone you can then turn towards shore and swim in. To survive you must stick to the rules and guidelines.

That's it, every day I seem to be panicking with irrational thoughts racing through my mind and fighting the rip current of events. I often fail to remember the simple rules of supporting a loved one with this disorder. I must be the one to remain calm and think clearly. I must be the one to remind Steph of the guiding principles that can be the best chance of surviving this rip current of a disorder. Again, it seems I am failing in my most sacred duty as a mother; to guide her cub to surviving on her own.

True self-reflecting is something that most people, if they are really honest, shy away from. It's a very hard and often painful task. I know I spend a lot of time in the stage of denial. Accepting the reality of what can't be changed seems to always be at the forefront of all my misgivings and just beyond my reach. How to make that giant leap always seems to be at the core of my struggle and often my response to that struggle begets the sin of self pity.

I've often discovered that when things get tough, it's best for me to get back to basics. And I've come to realize that the basics for me, is to focus on Mama's mantra of "things could be worse", in fact they have been much worse. So I recommit myself to "keep putting one foot in front of the other" and continue to pray that "this to shall pass". Then just maybe, I will be able to put this part of my impasse to rest. One day, I hope to be once more, more than just a Mom of a Bipolar.

CHAPTER 15   Summer 2005

As my grandson turns two, Steph find herself with another new job that is less than a mile from the apartment where she, her son, her father and stepmother live. She is quickly approaching the age limit that allows her to remain on her father's medical insurance. Being permanently employed is much more crucial now and I can hear the anxiety in her voice. She is at a make or break stage, losing this job would in many ways be tragic to her continued welfare on many levels.

This seems to be one of the biggest problems for people with mental illnesses. It's a vicious circle of needing to work to provide health insurance that will provide medications and treatment that enables a person to remain stable enough to keep working. The foundation of medications and doctors visits are just too crucial to their mental wellbeing yet are unfortunately just too expensive without insurance. If one brick comes loose, the wall easily falls down into a pile of rubble. Once the wall crumbles, it's very difficult, nearly impossible, for our loved one to rebuild the wall alone.

No matter what cracks periodically appear, Steph continues to prove to be a wonderful mother. Always attentive to my grandson's every need, monitoring his health and wellbeing like a pro. I have to acknowledge that being a mother doesn't seem to be the challenge, or detriment to her, I had once thought. Maybe just having a challenge that is bigger, more important that her self and her own crisis is what continues' to press her along. Maybe the challenge of being a mother is her saving grace after all. It figures, once again I should have listened to Mama.

With Dylan's asthma and allergies more under control than ever, he is quickly blossoming into a delightfully inquisitive little boy. None of the brain damage or neurological problems that were predicted at his birth has come true. He's proving to be a very clever, humorous and thoughtful; a completely normal little boy, something none of us thought we would ever be able to say.

I find nothing more entertaining than just watching the two of them interact. For me this seems to be the most surprising joy of being a grandmother, seeing the chain of love growing into that unbreakable bond. In those simple day to day observations I can see how parental love can conquer all, endure all. Isn't the circle of life and seeing what love can accomplish, an amazing thing?

As the weeks pass, Steph works hard to learn her new position. Finally, she has a job that doesn't entail answering phones and dealing with lots of people. This job seems perfect for her, sitting in a cubicle reviewing, organizing, correcting and adding data to client files in preparation for court proceedings. My little perfectionist is totally in her element.

This is where she shines. Steph is the epitome of organization and has an uncanny ability to streamline task. Without all the distractions and disruptions of phone calls or contact with customers, she quickly catches on to her assigned task. Soon Steph begins revamping her position, modifying and combining steps; she easily cuts wasted time out of her duties. This in turn, enables her manager to assign her more functions, which she also rapidly condenses with ease. It seems her manager could not be more pleased.

I don't know why I find myself surprised at her abilities, underneath her fragile mind, Steph is still a brilliant young lady; it's just been awhile since this aspect has had room to manifest itself. I find myself clinging to the hope that the snowball effect will have time to take hold. Weeks, then months pass quickly by as I hold my breath.

As I look back over time, I have to concede the unbelievable changes that Steph has made. I know the past six years has taken such a devastating emotional toll on her and how she sees herself, struggling with hopelessness and worthlessness from day to day. Though I still consider Steph to be somewhat mentally fragile, I'm taken aback by the transformation of late. I have to admit, she is handling motherhood and a good job better than I ever imagined possible.

As Steph's three month performance review approaches, a day which she rarely makes it past without a pink slip, another dilemma arises. Steph's father and stepmother decide to move to a new apartment, one that is an hour away from her new job. This hour does not include the twenty minutes she has to drive north to take Dylan to daycare. In view of her driving history and tendency to be late to work, this move is not an option that can practically be considered.

While I panic, Steph seems to take the news in stride. She simply says, "I'll just have to look for a cheap apartment." "I always knew this day would come, but I was hoping it would be when I made more money." Knowing Steph would not be able to afford an apartment on her current salary, Matt and I offer to help her. Settling on a budget the search begins with less than two months to secure an apartment.

Just a few days before her review, Steph calls me flooding the line with nervousness and alarm. As it turns out, this time her anxiety is born of relief and not from another disappointment. The company she works for had large layoffs that morning and yet she still has a job. I don't know who is more surprised, me or Steph.

Earlier in the day her manager had noticed how nervous she was as news of the layoffs began to spread through the building. Having a compassionate heart, she took Steph into her office and told her she need not worry. She was not letting such a productive and valuable employee go that easily. She explains about the layoffs and how the company was getting rid of some dead weight, something her boss didn't consider Steph being.

Though shook up by seeing the other's lose their jobs, Steph is encouraged beyond belief by these words of praise. Someone totally unrelated to her, thinks she is valuable and worthy. That thought surrounds her with a comforting blanket of hope.

Just one month after the layoffs, Steph and Dylan move into their own apartment. Though she considers her apartment to be in "Ghetto Ville", Steph also confides that it feels like they are living in a mansion. For almost three years she has lived with her Dad and Step mom in their small two bedroom apartment. The last two of those years has been spent sharing her room with her son. Having her own furniture and belongings out of storage and in a place she can now call her own, seems to give her a lift beyond compare.

Though our phone calls continue, usually daily, they soon become filled with discussions mostly about normal everyday stuff, co-worker issues and just the comical things Dylan is saying and doing. True some days Steph seems a little chattier than at others times, sometimes a little more subdued but nothing that sends the alarm bells ringing. After all this time, who would have thought I could ever call anything normal?

I've spent so many years of having to constantly be on guard against her drastic and frequent mood swings. The need I felt to always be judging and monitoring her stability over the phone has instilled in me the mind set that nothing could ever be normal again. Now, I find myself having a difficult time adjusting to these changes, its almost seems like I miss the chaos.

This thought brings back to my mind the theory I considered years ago of mind training and how repetition in a behavior can create and reinforce new patterns in our brains. While these repetitions seem to be proving beneficial for Steph and her continued stability, I can't boast of such positive results. For me, I have to admit the cycle of constantly being on guard and worrying has created some sort of negative pattern.

Sitting on the porch one day listening to another one of my vents, Matt comments that it's important to Steph that I find a way to let go of my fears, to stop looking for trouble. Concerned that my mindset could inhibit Steph from continued success; he says "you have to let her feel that you believe in her, that she can be normal". All those years of hearing Steph say "I don't want my life to be all about being Bipolar", has apparently not sunk in with me.

I've focused so much on trying to accept Steph's mental illness that it seems I have not let myself adjust to the apparent new and improved reality. I had no idea I was such an inflexible person, unable to adapt with the changes that are becoming more evident every day. Thinking about this for a while, I conclude that just maybe, this mindset is brought on by the fear that if I accept this new reality, I will fail in my duty of being the watchdog and miss some important warning signal.

As the months fly by, with a recommitment to the Serenity Prayer, I soon discover that I can let two or even three days pass without talking to Steph before I panic. Though I'm trying my best to loosen the apron strings a little, I must admit it's still difficult for me. It's certainly helpful to me when I periodically get a message from her, teasing me about how she hasn't heard from me in days and that she is worried about me. My, my... how the tables are turning.

225

This seems to be a big part of what is helping me relax somewhat, just hearing her sense of humor return. It's showing up with almost every phone call as she jokes about funny events at work or something funny Dylan has done. Humor and also, her renewed ability to express empathy about a friend that is having personal problems, these are all things that I have been missing for years.

I recently discovered another technique Steph has started using in times of stress. Whenever she feels herself getting frustrated or rattled by something, she stops, takes several deep breaths and just tells herself, "it will be okay, I can do this". While this is not a new discovery on her part, just a simple variation of one of Mama's secret tricks I've witnessed for years. Steph is beginning to remind me of Felix the Cat with her trusty bag of tricks.

I find I am continually amazed, even in the face of this serious mental illness, Steph chooses to actively search for the resources to help her retain stability. Searching for and choosing to use all the means available to her, medication, positive thinking, healthy lifestyle and seeking family support have all become the key to her continued path to success. She could have done as many others have in these same circumstances and just as easily have given up and said, to hell with it all. Somehow the inner core of Stephanie's determined spirit has never allowed herself to accept that mindset.

As I think of these thoughts, for some strange reason it brings to my mind a movie that I saw recently. In Will Smith's movie The Pursuit of Happyness at the end he reminisces about a portion of our countries Declaration of Independence. He reminds us of the fact that our creator, who made us all equal, endowed us with certain rights. He has given us, what our Founding Fathers and I as well, still believe to be our most valuable treasure, the right to Life, Liberty and the Pursuit of Happiness. I agree with this premise that sometimes we tend to forget that it's really important, to place an emphasis on the word "Pursuit". This one word, "Pursuit", is what makes the world of difference.

This simple word and the result of putting this very word into action by unrelenting determination, perseverance and sometimes sheer stubbornness, have certainly made a difference in both my children's life. The mind set that one must keep trying, must stay in the fight in spite of frustrating obstacles has, in itself brought them both to a place of happiness.

I've always tried to remember and practice those lessons Daddy taught me as a child, to work hard, play by the rules and to pay your own way. I just never really put it together that he was really talking about the principles of the constitution until now. I wonder how much better off our country would be if these lessons were more ingrained into the minds of all our young people these days.

With my children both doing so well; I couldn't be more proud of passing that mind set on to the next generation. Just the other day Phillip called to tell me some exciting news. Proving to be such a good mechanic and employee, his manager promoted him to team supervisor. Managing four other mechanics in his new position will provide a nice bonus each month based on the number of hours they work as a team. Since starting with the dealership, his salary has now increased seven dollars an hour.

In just five short years, my son has gone from a frustrated teen with no skills, not having a clue how he would support himself, to a man earning about seventy thousand dollars a year. In addition, he has accumulated over fifteen thousand dollars in tools and at any given time, owns three or four cars older cars that he buys cheap, refurbishes and repairs, then sells them for a profit. Apparently you don't have to be an academic to be industriously creative.

Not only is his financial situation now on firm ground. His very character would make any mother proud.

This quiet young man has now become the big brother to many young ladies; freely offering his mechanical services to those in need. He has grown into the type of guy who will stop after working all day to help a stranded motorist. He relishes in being a dependable friend who will actually show up to help someone move on his only day off. Nope, I couldn't be more proud for him and life he leads.

As for Steph, during this last year or so, I've watched her step by step, return more and more back into the vibrant young lady I once knew. For quite a while now she has maintained a normal weight. Being able to have those real heart to heart talks with her, laugh as well as cry with her, is an experience I hold dear to my heart again. Months can go by without the word Bipolar even being spoken between us. It's simply a word, just like diabetes or high blood pressure. It no longer rules our lives.

I've come to the conclusion that the word "accept" has been a detriment to me in my ability to deal with my daughter's mental illness. I wasted an enormous amount of energy struggling with the feelings and emotions brought about by my lack of acceptance. In the beginning of Steph's illness, I failed to accept that something was wrong. Then I let myself be tormented over the inability to accept that her life had forever been changed.

As I forced myself to accept who she had become, if find that that particular word often inhibited me from believing that she could have any success in her life. Even as I saw her rally, out of sheer determination, to make it in this world in spite of her illness, I seem to refuse to accept that she can ever attain her goal.

Over and over I have struggled and fought with this word. This word has, in a way paralyzed me, stifled and hindered my capacity for being the support Steph needed. No longer, do I believe I must "accept" a situation though; our minds are too powerful and flexible to be put into such a rigid concept. I continue to practice Mama's secrets though I must

228

admit I haven't yet mastered the art. I guess in a way, I have just decided to put the word "accept" in a box on a shelf in the far corner of my closet. Maybe one day my brain will understand what to do with this word.

Experts say we only use about ten percent of our brains abilities. If this is true, then we must acknowledge that we have a great untouched capacity to achieve unfathomable greatness and the ability to overcome insurmountable difficulties. If we could find a way to tap into the other ninety percent, maybe we would find ourselves with the ability to cure any disease just with the power of our own thought.

Our thoughts it seems are often what get in our way, our fears and doubts and yes, even the very idea of acceptance is what sometimes keeps us from achieving our goals. Again we see the power of words, what a tangled web we can create in our minds, just by the use of them. We all feel the pain of those unwanted words the moment they pop into our heads.

I have often wondered where Steph would be now if she had given into the many words that have plagued her for so many years. Giving into worthlessness, hopelessness and despair or allowing the wild crazy ideas to take total control over her could have destroyed her. Though at times, each of these words definitely had a grip on her; she has fought them stubbornly and refuses to allow them to continue to rule her life.

With this thought in mind, I must admit that Steph in many ways seems mentally healthier than I do. At least in inner strength, I'm sure she has outshined me on all points. Maybe it's just her insightful, intuitive, determined part of her mind that still exists and struggles to overcome her illness. Apparently, being Bipolar doesn't dissolve the inner brilliance of the mind.

I can't even express in mere words the amount of joy that fills my heart, as I see both my children, after facing very different but trying circumstances, come into their own as adults. Being a mother, though it has always been such a marvelous experience for me, it has also come with overwhelming amount of worries and despair. I continue to struggle with enormous amounts of guilt, confusion and anger that swell up inside me, often making me feel paralyzed just from the shear weight of them.

Arriving at this place in my life, it has now left me with such a strange mixture of pent up conflicting feelings, I find myself with a need to somehow sort them out before I can put them away forever in a box. This need has lead to a quest for some form of therapy that would provide an outlet for all those scattered emotions that are bottled up inside me.

And so here we are at last, in the midst of my chosen therapy. I have poured my heart out, struggled to be frank and honest, cried rivers of tears as I relived my inner turmoil over my daughters mental illness. Though I still have many more questions than answers, still struggle with the unfairness of it all, I have in many ways, finally allowed myself to just take some of Steph's advice. After all is said and done I have simply chosen to a deep breath and made the decision to not let being the mother of a Bipolar to rule my life. Finally now I can get on with, just being Mom.

CHAPTER 16 Summer 2008

We live in a country where millions of men and
women are diagnosed with some form of a mental illness. A
vast majority of them are our nation's young people, with
many more yet to reach out for the help they will need for the
remainder of their lives. During the turn of this century,
health professionals have diagnosed mental illnesses of
monumental proportion.

Is this a new phenomenon or has our mental health
professionals recently made such astounding breakthroughs
in the diagnosis of mental health issues? Has society's
awareness increased in this realm so dramatically these last
20 years? We would all have to agree, the last few
generations have seen remarkable progress in this most
difficult issue.

With great hope and the dedication of brilliant
psychiatrist and neurological specialist, the twenty-first
century will bring unfathomable new discoveries in the
workings of the mind. Also we, as a society, no longer are
shutting our eyes to hard truths, hiding our loved ones away
and turning our backs on them.

Looking back throughout history, psychiatrist can
recognize hundreds of famous people who they believe
suffered from a mental disorder. Many of our homeless are
stricken with a mental disorder that continues to go untreated.
Do we really believe people in their right mind would want to
choose that lifestyle? Most likely, there has always been a

larger population throughout the years with mental health issues than has been documented.

Some of them we might recognize within our own nucleus of friends and families, with a possible undiagnosed illnesses. The aunt or uncle that was always so much fun to us kids, but mom and dad never appreciated their odd grasp on life, the cousin who never could hold down a job because of his extreme moodiness. Maybe the neighbor who always had these really wild exciting ideas, you know, the kind that makes you shake your head & go "wow, what were they thinking"? What about the friend that disappears for days or weeks, even months on end, then reappears like they have the world on a string?

If you have chosen to read this book, more than likely you or someone in your life is struggling with a mental illness. You have probably already been searching for statistics and medical journals in your own quest for direction, so I have chosen not duplicate their data. Though the information is profoundly helpful, my goal has been to focus on the effects of this tragedy on myself and my family.

While I fully admit, I am not an expert by any means on mental illnesses; there are a few things I have come to accept as necessary in the management of my daughter's continued stability and those who fall prey to these illnesses. I can only hope that my experiences and suggestions are helpful.

Experts agree that there is an unequivocal need to be under continual care of a trusted qualified psychiatrist. The importance of taking the prescribed medication is crucial. And as difficult and frustrating as it can be, struggling through the trial and error period is just as important. Finding the medications that work for each individual case and taking them for the remainder of their life is the first and foremost component to stability.

Monitoring and practicing good general health such as eating, exercising, sleeping regularly and maintaining a calm, low stress atmosphere can make a huge difference. If you question this, just remember the last time you stayed up all night or went through a full day without eating and then tried to work productively. What mind can think clearly under any of these conditions?

I have shared frequently certain phrases that my family has used throughout my life to encourage, strengthen, inspire and even sustain us, in times of crisis. Speaking aloud these and many other such uplifting words can be a powerful tool that I highly recommend practicing. We have the luxury of an expansive and expressive vocabulary, freely available to us. I implore you to find those meaningful words that work for you and speak them often.

Many may think that just staying on their meds is all, that people suffering from Bipolar Disorder needs to remain stable. While this is a crucial part of their treatment, I find that these other aspects are equally important. For some there may be other means that help them. Be open minded, the key is finding those practices that will work best for you and them.

We all seem to thrive when we have others in our live to lean on in times of need. Without a doubt, those with a mental illness need a solid support system, people that will commit to monitoring, encouraging, emotional support. And yes, even step in and take control when needed, when the pendulum swings too far out of balance. It takes a solid commitment of trust between the supporter as well as those who need that crucial support. This is always easier said than done.

Finally, I would encourage those, who chose to be the support system of our mentally ill, to put your frustrations down to paper. By expressing those thoughts and feelings of anger, despair, confusion and heartache in a written form has been an invaluable coping mechanism for me. Though it has

233

not solved all my woes, it has brought great relief to my troubled mind.

Whether you chose to share your tale with others, as I have, or not, does not matter. Just performing this simple process can help release those bottled up emotions, emotions that can easily overwhelm you. Keeping yourself in a stable frame of mind is imperative to your continued ability to being that all important support system for your loved one.

As I look back over the last nine years, I have often wondered about the many mothers and fathers that are out there who have walked this turbulent and heart wrenching path. Feeling all the joys as I have, watching a child's life blossoming into a promising adulthood, only to face the desperation that comes with seeing that dear child fall prey to the torment of mental illness. The helplessness a parent feels in this situation, knowing there is nothing you can do to take this away from them, is an experience I know I could have lived without.

Yet there is a part of me that can now step back and appreciate the experience, for without living through this, I would not see my daughter as the amazing person she has proven to be. In my mind she will always be my champion, someone who I admire just for her sheer determination, courage and strength.

Daddy once told me as he faced his own struggle with cancer that you must play the cards life deals to you. I think this has been my greatest challenge; accepting that though the cards didn't seem fair, I could not just fold my hand. I can't tell you how many times, I felt like just cashing in my chips and storming off, saying "I don't want to play anymore". But then who really does want to play this particular game? Thankfully, Stephanie continues to play her hand and it is with some measure of shame I must say, her bravery is what encourages me to stay in the game.

I often think of all the things I'm thankful for. I am thankful that I had parents who taught traditions and values that fostered the spirit of determination, perseverance, keeping all things in perspective and the necessity of maintaining a positive attitude. Thankful that those things were stressed so strongly, that those same principles seemed important enough for me to instill them in my own children's mind and heart. The difference those ideals continue to make in our lives are invaluable.

I am thankful to live in this country, in a time that the scientific community and our medical professionals have a better understanding of the workings of our complicated minds. Without the treatments that are now available, I can't imagine what it would be like, facing such serious mental illnesses. I am deeply encouraged by the prospects of their future discoveries.

I am thankful for my husband, Matt, who swooped into my life at just the right moment. Without his insight and perception, who knows how long it would have taken me to realize the gravity of the situation and get Steph the help she needed. Having his strength, comfort and patience during those turbulent years, was the sole reason I was able to do as Mama always encouraged me to do; to keep putting one foot in front of the other.

Most of all, I am thankful every day of my life, for the birth of my grandson, Dylan. I believe without reservation, he is the source of Steph's determination and strength. She will look anyone, square in the eye and contribute her continued stability to her need to be the best Mama Bear she can be. Though I'm not saying that all young ladies with a mental illness should get pregnant, but I do believe there is a need to have something or someone in their lives, that opens their eyes to the reality of just how extremely important their stability and continued well being truly is.

As in Stephanie's case, her son seems to be the catalyst that brought her to the realization of just how important her emotional stability is for herself, but more importantly for her son. The wisdom of what Mama told me of all those years ago proclaiming Dylan as her "Saving Grace has definitely rung true. In Steph's own words "it's not just about me anymore."

I feel so fortunate to also have now come to a place, when someone asks me about my daughter, I can smile and say "she's doing great". While this is not really the end of my story, I do know that it is time to get on with learning how to live my own life again.

Even though in the back of my mind there will always remain the possibility, the likelihood, that Steph will have other bouts of instability, I am grateful to know that it could have been worse, a lot worse and for the moment anyway, "that this too has passed."

I know in my heart of hearts that many other stories out there that need to be told, that there are many, much more tragic experiences than Steph's. Many of our nation's young people have not found a way to climb out of the pit of despair and are in desperate need of our help and support.

We have seen in recent years, what can happen when our mentally ill loved ones, cross that delicate line into instability and psychosis. Often they take their own lives, but sometimes they take other innocent victims with them, as we saw a few years ago in the Virginia Tech tragedy.

I've always thought of myself as a person inclined to believe that black is black, white is white, right is right and wrong is wrong. But after living through this experience with my daughter, life has taught me that there are often shades of grey that must be acknowledged and considered. The answers and solutions for these tragic situations can not be, so easily defined. I believe it is a responsibility we have, as a society, to look out for those in our families and communities, whose minds are in such turmoil and disarray.

One last tidbit of joy I must share with you. My last trip home, I leave for the airport ecstatic. This particular trip home is special because I bring with me the news that Matt and I are moving home. My joy is ripe with anticipation as I meet my daughter in the parking lot where she has worked for four years now.

At this company, she has thrived earning three promotions and over twelve dollars an hour in raises. Standing next to my car waiting for her to come out, I hear an excited "Mom!" As I turn around, Steph's radiant smile and glistening hair catches my eye. Confidently she hurries towards me in an adorable size eight business outfit, almost skipping as she tries to contain her joy.

As she reaches me, she throws her arms around my neck, giving me a hug that simply takes my breath away. It's seems like a lifetime ago since I have felt her arms so tightly around me. I've often heard it said "life really is about the little things". This may seem to some like such a little thing, but to me, seeing her this way, feelings those precious arms so tightly around me, meant that my daughter is really the one who has finally come home.

AKNOWLEDGEMENTS

The writing of this book though one of the more difficult accomplishments of my life, has proven to be great therapy for me. I could not have completed this without the support and help of many people.

First of all, I must thank my daughter, Stephanie and son, Phillip, for allowing me to expose our lives and experiences so openly. Without you both, my life would have been very empty. You both have filled me with joy and pride.

I give my most heartfelt thanks to my husband, Matt, for his patient understanding in the writing of this book. The months and months it took to write this could not have been suffered through without your support, guidance, and the relentless push to get this published. Without you and your steadfast guidance and support, this would probably be a very different story. You will forever be my soft place to fall.

Much admiration and appreciation goes to my mother, Katherine Wilson. Your continual wisdom and encouragement has inspired and sustained all of us for a lifetime. Your unique perception of life that you have shared so freely has made "The" difference in my struggle to look on the bright side.

Many thanks go to my sisters, Brenda Willis and Linda Abercromie for their helpful insight, suggestions, edits and support. You both are very dear to me.

To Aunt Junie and Uncle Jack Shea who inspire everyone they come in contact with to shoot for the stars and follow your dreams. Love ya, Love ya, Love ya.

To Liz Ritter who helped edit this work and gave me the courage to just go for it. Thanks to Jon Goodspeed for the direction and advice that lead to this printing. The help and encouragement you both provided has been immeasurable.

Finally to Dylan, there will never be enough words to express the love and joy you have brought into our lives.

Made in the USA
Lexington, KY
23 December 2009